ears
to
hear

50 YEARS OF
SAMARITAN
LISTENING

HILARY FORREST

SEDJEM PRESS, MANCHESTER

First published 2003

Published by Sedjem Press

1, Monaco Drive, Manchester M22 4FG

ISBN 0-9545114-0-9

All rights reserved

The moral right of the author has been asserted

Extracts and pictures by kind permission of the copyright holders

Typeset in 12pt Garamond

Designed by Deborah Cole

Printed by Delmar Press

*This book is dedicated to all those caring volunteers,
past and present, who have given so generously and
freely of their time and have listened for so many
hours to those who have turned to The Samaritans for
help in their times of crisis over the last 50 years.*

Acknowledgements

This book could not have been written without the support of my family and many friends. The following have given generously of their time to prepare the work for publication. Thanks to:

Isabel Arnold for legal advice.

Isabel Blincow for her delightful illustrations on pages 51, 60, 61 62, 66, 70, 72, 74, 78, 79, 84, 87.

Cartoon on page 18 by kind permission of John Forrest.

Sheila Coggrave for reading through the early drafts.

Elisabeth Salisbury for permission to draw on 'The Samaritan' freely and for copy-editing the piece.

Deborah Cole.

Mike Sherratt for reading the proofs.

Grateful thanks are given (in alphabetical order) to David Arthur, Kathy and Bill Baker, Mike Charman, Jenny Cunnington, John Eldrid, Joan Guénault, Albert Jewell, Norman Keir, Nancy Kerr, Jane Lowe, Pauline Roberts and Nat Smith, each of whom has given practical help.

Particular thanks to Wendy Parr and Beris Hudson whose help and encouragement were responsible for getting the project off the ground and for sustaining it throughout.

Preface

A household name for the past five decades, The Samaritans, the organisation which has traditionally offered befriending and support to those in despair or in danger of taking their own lives, has never had a comprehensive account written of its history and development. The story of its beginnings has been told many times, especially in the published works of its founder, the Reverend Dr Chad Varah, and various aspects of the work it has done are also a matter of record. In the 50th year of its existence, this small book is an attempt to present a straightforward record of its evolution. Inevitably there will be gaps. The whole idea of attempting to cover the history of an organisation with over 200 branches in Britain and Ireland alone and an average volunteer force of nearly 18,000, is both daunting and fascinating by turns. An apology must be offered to those readers who feel that *their* bit of the history has been omitted or cut short. The author received material from many sources which has had to be composed into a manageable narrative, without giving too much space to one particular aspect.

This is not intended to be an academic study or an analysis of the work, but rather an account of the founding, growth and development of The Samaritans as well as a record of some of the major issues which have preoccupied its members over the years. It is an unofficial record seen through the eyes of a long-standing volunteer.

The first section traces, in roughly chronological order the period from the setting up of the centre at St Stephen Walbrook in London in 1953, through the spread throughout Britain, Ireland and the world (though the space given to this last is more limited than it deserves, because of the scale of the work), its incorporation as a movement and the formalisation of its structure. This spans the first 20 or so years.

The second section, which covers roughly the late 60s, the 70s and the early 80s, deals with a range of issues which have concerned the movement and which have eventually been incorporated into the mainstream of Samaritan thinking. These include such matters as the relationship with the professions, training issues, and some questions of law as well as debates on sex and suicide.

The third section breaks with the chronological pattern for a while and consists of memories and experiences of real volunteers, many of them alarming and some amusing.

Back on the chronological track, the section spanning the 80s and 90s traces the change in Samaritan activity, covering the work done outside the branch through reaching out to vulnerable members of the community.

The final section is intended to outline the current position at the time of writing. The new telephone technologies which have allowed the single number and easy transfers of lines from one centre to another, the increasing importance of the e-mail service and a new evaluation by the movement of its role, all pose questions for the future. Where will things be in 50 years time?

Many thanks are extended to all those branches and individual volunteers who sent in information. I hope I have mentioned all of you in the text if not by name, at least by information. Grateful thanks also to the colleagues and friends too numerous to name individually who have given me the courage to produce this book, and especially those who have helped in practical ways by offering financial support or by reading the drafts and sharing their thoughts.

Although every effort has been been made to trace owners of copyright material the author apologises for any inadvertent infringement.

Note on Confidentiality
Although the incidents recorded did happen, some of the details have been changed or omitted to protect the confidentiality of callers.

HILARY FORREST, 2003

Chairmen of The Samaritans

CHAD VARAH
THE FOUNDER AND FIRST CHAIRMAN
without whose vision and inspiration The Samaritans
would never have come into being.

BILL THOMSON, Belfast 1966-1968
Bill Thomson founded the Belfast branch in 1961. He was the first to become chairman after Chad in 1966.

"The strains and stresses of the early days were smoothed by the quiet common sense and puckish charm of Bill Thomson. To take over from Chad was challenge enough, but to earn the love…and the respect of all the Samaritans was a tribute to his essential genius."

His greatest achievement was the setting up of the Irish region which to this day transcends all political or sectarian divides. His early death robbed the movement of a great servant.

JOHN ELDRID, Portsmouth and CLB 1968-1972
"My contribution to Samaritans is a mixture of volunteer and professional roles. My initiation began when I was working as an assistant priest to Chad in London 1958-

1964. This was followed by further education as a volunteer-director of Portsmouth branch for eight years, co-director of Festival branch and 13 years as director of central London branch.

These experiences have given me special encounters with thousands of callers and hundreds of volunteers. I am convinced Samaritan befriending by telephone, and especially face to face is an essential source of human warmth. This helps to melt the ice of those freezing to death in their despair. Befriending is unique and is an essential factor in reducing the risk of suicide for many; professional help is also essential. My message to Samaritans is 'remember the suicidal and despairing need access to all possible options. Wise befriending can open all kinds of apparently closed doors'."

DAVID ARTHUR, Edinburgh, Aberdeen, Correspondence 1972-1976

"I became a Samaritan, untrained, in 1956 as a result of an article of Chad's. I joined because I felt that here was an opportunity to offer help to desperate people in a most practical and effective way. What attracted me to Samaritan befriending was what also took me into teaching, hands-on/ear-on directly to other human beings. Because it presented an enormous challenge, on the phone or face to face, it was up to you to succeed or fail. There was no clutter of rules, just two human beings looking for resolution by trying to be a human being. It also attracted me that there was always a warmth and humour wherever there were Samaritans. Chad's great idea caught one of those 'moments in the tides of men'."

MICHAEL YORKE, Chelmsford 1976-1979

"Being chairman of the Samaritans was one of the most formative experiences of my life. It gave me the opportunity, at a comparatively early age, to be at the heart of a growing and developing charity that in so many ways was breaking new ground in the care of troubled people. It gave me the opportunity to chair large meetings of highly competent and committed groups of people who, as the Council of Management or the Executive, provided policy leadership to

the branches. The other great gift for me was a set of long-standing friends with whom I am still in contact even though I left the movement 15 years ago."

Now Dean of Lichfield, Michael continues with the following message. *"Like many callers, I have so much for which to be grateful to The Samaritans; and I hope, in a very changed environment the branches will continue to deliver a personal and committed service to all who turn to them for help. Go well, my friends!"*

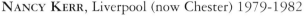

NANCY KERR, Liverpool (now Chester) 1979-1982
"When you become chair of the Samaritans, your caring and listening to callers and fellow volunteers extends from your own locality to all branches. The key volunteers are those on duty, and you are there to support them. So, you are at the bottom rung of the Samaritan ladder - not the top."

NAT SMITH, Teesside 1982-1985
"Being chairman was an amazing experience. One had joined the Samaritans to sit quietly in a corner listening to a single person and now one was expected to talk to many. One talked, and even preached to hundreds of volunteers and members of the public. All the time one had to remind oneself that it was as a temporary representative of 2,300 other volunteers. The support of the nine paid staff at Slough was magnificent. I have never felt such strong team spirit as at that time in The Samaritans."

ALBERT JEWELL, Leeds 1985-1987
"Chairing the Council of Management was quite daunting. During my time there were heated debates on double manning and mandatory on-going training. Branch directors are rightly passionate in fighting for what they see as the central values of our work.
The camaraderie of the Executive Committee was about as good as it gets. It was a real privilege to be so close to our president, Doris Odlum - so old, so wise, so practical - to meet Chad on many occasions and to rub shoulders with our various consultants who without exception were colourful, highly able and totally dedicated to the cause of befriending the suicidal."

NORMAN KEIR, Teesside 1987-1990

"Being made national chairman provides an opportunity to serve our callers in a rewarding role no more exacting than that of being a branch director or rota secretary. It is a privileged position which enables one to see our organisation as a whole and so to realise how everything we do is dependent on the efforts and skills of our members. Without in any way denigrating the excellent support given by the staff at general office, it is fair to say that one of the strengths of the Samaritans is that at all levels it is run by volunteers."

SHEILA COGGRAVE, Sunderland 1990-1993

"The chairman's role is complex, demanding and challenging. It would be surprising if anyone felt equal to it but it is comforting to have such a network of support from so many other volunteers and of course from staff. This underpins our work for callers and permeates the movement. Every chairman must balance necessary leadership with being the servant of the Council and of the wider movement. That requires listening, treating everyone with respect and remembering that if they don't feel valued or appreciated volunteers can vote with their feet."

JENNY CUNNINGTON, Bradford 1993-1996

"During my time as chairman, I was chatting to fellow volunteers during my weekly shift in my branch, Bradford. The conversation turned to national guidelines. One colleague said, 'perhaps you'd know something about this, Jenny. You do something outside the branch, don't you? Aren't you president or something?' I think this highlights so beautifully the basic premise of our role as Samaritans. We are all, first and foremost, volunteers, doing weekly shifts on the phone, and if some of us care to travel beyond the branch, then fine, someone has got to do it. But to me, the strength of our volunteer-led movement is that every one of us who undertakes national tasks is kept in touch with what we are all about, our callers."

John Lawrie, Edinburgh 1996-1999

"Being chairman was immensely rewarding and a huge honour. It was also a curious mixture - carrying the responsibility for steering a major charity in the right direction on one hand with the opportunity for regular and direct contact with Samaritans and branches on the other. As vice-chair and chair I visited 84 of the 203 branches often having to fit ingenious travel arrangements (invariably by public transport) around the demands of the day job."

Bernard Finnemore, Stoke 1999-2002

During his chairmanship Bernard oversaw the process of consultation which was known as *Facing the future* and on which the current changes in emphasis and image are based.

Daphne Pullen, South West Herts 2002-

In the beginning

As a child of the vicarage I was often aware of serious matters being discussed by my elders, many concerning parishioners. I vividly remember Mrs X, a lady of slightly eccentric appearance whose two daughters, my contemporaries, always followed rather primly two paces behind. One day I heard that Mrs X had been *"carted off to the local mental hospital"*, (people were not quite so sensitive in their use of language then). I particularly recall the feeling I had when I heard that she had even been deprived of her hairpins in case she harmed herself. I had this vision of her, wild-eyed and straggle-haired and felt very much aware even at that early age of this encroachment on her dignity. After her discharge she did indeed harm herself - by putting her head in the gas oven, the commonest method of killing oneself in those days. It was my first brush with suicide and made a great impression. By coincidence in that same year, 1953, a London rector, Chad Varah began to offer a telephone line to those who were desperate or suicidal. Curiously, I remember my father commenting on this over breakfast one day, as the rector's name was one well known to us, as we had been avid readers of *The Eagle,* to which Chad had been a regular contributor, since its first issue.

The factors which led up to the creation of The Samaritans are a matter of record. Chad Varah has outlined them many times in various forms, including his autobiography. Social attitudes before and just after the Second World War were very different from those of the early years of the 21st century. There were many taboos. Children often remained ignorant of matters which were embarrassing to their parents, who, raised in the Victorian or post-Victorian eras, could not bring themselves to discuss such matters as sex. There are still people alive today who experienced unconsummated marriages because they simply did not know what to do. It was probably this kind of inhibition which helped to cause the tragedy which was one of the factors which eventually led to the Samaritan line being set up. As a young curate, Chad had conducted a burial service for a young girl who had killed herself because she had not been told about menstruation and thought she had some shameful disease. The death itself was bad enough but Chad recalls that the burial was conducted outside consecrated ground, the judgement of society on suicide, the second great taboo. This death made an impression on the young man and he decided from then on to wage a personal war on sexual ignorance. This became a lifelong crusade.

Think of a number

After a number of changes of job including becoming involved in journalism, Chad arrived in the London area. His contacts in Fleet Street allowed him to write many published articles including, in 1953, one in the popular magazine *Picture Post* on the sexual difficulties which might be faced by both men and women during the course of their lives. Scores of people wrote to him saying that he had released them from their darkness and given them back their self-respect. In some cases extreme feelings of guilt had driven them to the brink of suicide. At that time the guilt was further compounded by the fact that they knew they would be committing a crime by killing themselves. Some sought personal interviews with Chad. At the time he was leading a busy life as a parish priest and could see no way of following this up. He is on record as saying that he issued a kind of challenge to God and very shortly afterwards was offered the living of St Stephen Walbrook, a London City church with few actual parishioners. This was his chance to act.

He set up in the church vestry. The story of his ringing up the GPO to ask for a suitably memorable number for his phone is a strange one. Amid the dust and debris left behind by the blitz there was a telephone. He used this to make his request, suggesting that a good number would be MANsion House (the local exchange) 9000. *"Where are you calling from?"*, asked the operator. He cleared the dust from the dial only to reveal *"MANsion House 9000"*. That original phone is to be seen to this day in a glass case at St Stephen's, where it all began. The first calls were dealt with by the rector, helped by his secretary, Vivien, but soon there were visitors as well. Sometimes they had to wait a long time to see the rector so various lay-people were recruited to welcome them. It was then that the real Samaritan idea was born. Chad says himself that the true date of the foundation of The Samaritans was February 1954 when he said to his volunteer force *"over to you"*. He often claimed that he never answered the phone after this but of course he did, frequently being the only person on the premises. From then on, he saw the *special clients*, those with particular, often sexual, difficulties while the volunteers answered the

Chad with the original phone

telephone. He had realised that some of his clients, instead of waiting to see him had gone away apparently with a lighter heart having chatted with the tea-makers. From this the special Samaritan idea of *befriending* developed. The tea-makers became the accepting, non-judgmental warm human contact of which many of those distressed people had urgent need. The relief of sharing dark thoughts and what they felt were shameful secrets was enormously important. After all, at that time depression was hardly recognised by most people. Sufferers were admonished to *"pull themselves together"* or to *"snap out of it"*. Other forms of mental illness were spoken of in hushed tones. Suicide was not only viewed as a sin, but was against the law. Some found their despair at

Chad in his office at St Stephen's in the 50s

not being successful in ending their lives compounded by finding themselves in court for having attempted it.

It was not originally the Founder's idea to use the term *Samaritan*. Its obvious religious connotation was not exactly in step with his intention, (though of course the point of the parable is that the original Samaritan was an outsider of the religious society whose members had all *"passed by on the other side"*). It was the press who first coined the name, calling Chad *"the Samaritan priest"* and his line *"the telephone good Samaritans"*. In fact his many journalistic friends ensured that the location and the phone number were widely publicised in the national press. In later days there were debates about the name. Alternatives were offered but always using the epithet *Samaritan*. Many new branches when they set up called themselves the *Telephone Samaritans* and when the organisation was incorporated as a company limited by guarantee, the *Company* of Samaritans was suggested. It was decided in the end to keep it simple, though from time to time there have been suggestions that in the name of *corporate image* the name should be completely changed. Fortunately a recent *rebranding* has only adjusted the name slightly by dropping the definite article.

For six years St Stephen's was the only group in the country until a centre was launched in Edinburgh in 1959. The original members were also a very mixed group, belonging to different religions, or to none and covering a wide spectrum of experience, both professional and amateur. It was their common humanity and warmth, coupled with the ability to listen which created the group's identity. The Founder had absolute power in the running of the group. He laid down rules which had to be obeyed and was even known to dismiss members summarily on occasion without having to explain why. He insisted that the client always came first. Nowadays those who seek help are referred to

A Monday meeting in the 50s (On the left is Jean Burt who later became one of the general secretaries at Slough)

as *callers* since the word *client* was thought to smack too much of the professional services.

Those early volunteers used to take their sandwiches along at lunchtime on a Monday to meet each other and talk. The available space was very small and had to be shared with such practical objects as a stepladder and the ceiling consisted of strips of hessian, an emergency solution to war damage, but the feeling of team spirit was fostered by these sessions. The meetings were the forerunners of what Samaritans call nowadays *Preparation*. Volunteers listened to No. 1, Chad, and discussed issues which concerned them. According to one of these, No. 78, they learnt *"the importance of listening, hearing what the client was trying to say"*. Things were amazingly formal in those days. Although duty volunteers signed themselves in the daily log only by their number, clients generally not only gave their full names but often their address as well. Apparently anonymity only stretched one way. One of the original pegboards with plastic numerals showing the numbers of one of the last shifts to be worked there still exists in the crypt, though the branch is long gone.

Part of the last week's rota at St Stephen's as it is today

Tales from the crypt

To Samaritan volunteers outside the capital in the 1960s the London branch had its own aura of mystery. The idea of a Samaritan centre situated in the crypt of a famous City church carried a kind of romance, especially amongst those who were working in their own extraordinarily uncomfortable circumstances. In fact for the first ten years there was no crypt, or rather, no crypt was known. It was only in the early 60s that the rector noticed a trap in the floor after some old flooring had been removed. He took a torch and crawled down under the church to see what was there. This seems to have been a remarkably risky operation as no-one knew what he was up to. It ended in the triumphant discovery of a huge space full of mouldering coffins which was subsequently cleared in an operation which would make modern archaeologists blench. There was no anxiety about possible germs nor any consideration of health and safety precautions such as those observed in the 1980s in a similar operation at Christ Church, Spitalfields. The crypt was made into a spacious new Samaritan Centre. It seems nobody ever found it spooky, despite the coffins piled up and walled into a corner. Perhaps the occupants approved of what their space was being used for.

The Central London branch remained in the crypt, increasingly cramped as the operation expanded until its move, first to Kensington, then to its present premises in Marshall Street in the middle of Soho in October 1987.

In those early days, Chad was inclined to use any offer of help immediately. One potential volunteer who had gone to see him about joining in the work found himself being sent off to a suburban railway station to talk to a very distressed man who happened, at that moment to be speaking to the rector on the phone. One can imagine how unprepared the volunteer must have felt but he has stuck with Samaritan work for the last 40-odd years.

At first the hours were limited. By 1956 there were sufficient volunteers to cover the hours of 6 till 10 pm but there was no thought of covering the night. When this came it was an eerie experience for the first overnight volunteer, (44). It took place on New Year's Eve, a time when it was thought there might be a need. In fact, *"waiting in a dark church in the makeshift surroundings of a bombed vestry with the deserted city outside"* was a somewhat unnerving experience. The phone rang several times, but each call was only a fellow-volunteer offering encouragement.

From the very earliest days the work was often more practical than it is now.

One former volunteer at Walbrook, Frank, who now belongs to a different London branch was once asked by No.1 to take in a prostitute who was trying to break with her former life-style. He agreed and she stayed at his home for more than a week until accommodation could be found for her well outside London.

According to John Eldrid who was involved very early on in the London branch specialised in *"supporting homosexuals and other fugitives from the law"*. There was also a strong emphasis on helping to provide a safe haven for those who needed one. A house at Marney Road was donated in which there were six emergency beds. These were in constant use and many a distressed person found refuge. In later years the Samaritan organisation has, in general, become much less pro-active but the London branch to this day inclines to follow the old way to some extent. It is not uncommon to call in doctors or other experts to see callers where other branches tend to use their consultants as advisors in the background. A study of the annual reports of the branch in the 60s and early 70s gives an impressive list of consultants on psychiatry, religion, the law and much else. Many of those listed were at the top of their professions and included the then Archbishop of Canterbury. There are those, like John, and others who have worked with him in the past, who tend to regret the altered emphasis though

Chad in the same office in 2000

change was perhaps inevitable as the demand for the service grew. Realistically there are limits on the resources of voluntary organisations and some priorities have to be set.

In those early days it was expected that Chad himself would conduct the *special* interviews but as time went on the demands upon him became too great and others, like John Eldrid were recruited to help. There was also a kind of hierarchy in the branch where some volunteers, chosen by No. 1 became *Companions*. This is clearly shown in Monica Dickens' book, *The Listeners*, based on her own experience as a London volunteer. She was later to become the founder of the first American branch in Boston, Mass. In some provincial branches in the early days there was also a tradition of *special* interviews being conducted by the director. Manchester volunteers of the period well remember George, the vicar of the church in whose premises the branch was based rushing in, with his cassock and surplice flying out behind him, to see Miss Z who had a regular appointment with him for spiritual and perhaps psychological guidance.

This distinction between different *ranks* of Samaritan began to die out by the mid-60s and some branches, such as Guildford were quite outspoken in their belief in the equality of all volunteers.

"We see ourselves as strictly non-professional, ordinary people offering friendship to those whose lives are in a muddle...We do not condescend to helpers or canonise companions. On duty we are all Samaritans. We do not even call each other by our Christian names unless we would do so naturally without presumption and with common courtesy. A Samaritan on duty IS the branch...this privilege and responsibility is justified by careful selection at the start. Our director and the leaders (all active clergy) only rarely themselves conduct an interview. Surely if expert help is needed this is the moment for bringing the client in touch, if he agrees, with real professionals."

Two clues to the date of this quotation are noticeable. The strong influence of the clergy and the fact that first names were not necessarily used show that this was written in the 60s or early 70s. In fact the date is 1970. Nowadays it would be unthinkable for minutes of national, regional and local meetings to record the doings of Mr B, Mrs G or, (very frequently) Rev. J. Indeed in some branches surnames are all but forgotten even though working in contexts outside the branch has rendered the emphasis on anonymity less rigid.

St Stephen Walbrook

Wider still...

The work at St Stephen's remained unique until 1959 but the word began to get around, not least because of the personal efforts of the Founder. Around 1956 a dramatised programme was broadcast on Radio Luxembourg, at that time very popular with the young, and articles appeared often in the press. In 1958 the *Scotsman* published an article in which an appeal was made for anyone interested in the work to write in to Chad at St Stephen's. At least three Scots did so, including David Arthur, a schoolmaster, who later became chairman in the national arena. Shortly afterwards David was approached by Chad to deal with a problem. A Scottish client of Chad's had, sadly, killed himself and, in the custom of the time, been refused burial in consecrated ground. Naturally his widow was devastated; could David help? Having solved the burial problem, he began negotiations as a result of which Chad went to Edinburgh and met a number of interested parties including several notable local clergy, among them Jim Blackie, who was to become the first chairman of the new Edinburgh Samaritan branch. A public meeting was held to which about 60 people came. This number was eventually whittled down to around 40 and the group was ready to begin the process of setting up. A series of lectures was arranged by Rev. Jim Blackie through his university contacts, and the volunteers were ready to begin.

From the outset there were a number of problems. Premises were needed if there was to be a viable operation. The suggestion that Jim Blackie's church should be the site of the new centre did not go down well with Jim's wife, Nancy, so further search had to be made. Eventually a dusty and disused church hall, St Andrew's, on Queen Street was found. The early volunteers mopped out with enthusiasm and were quite prepared to put up with somewhat spartan conditions.

Another problem was the name to use. In Scotland there was already an organisation called *The Samaritans*, a kind of charitable trust which had been founded about 1860. Their prior claim to the title meant that in Scotland *The Telephone Samaritans* was the usual name in the early days. As the movement spread, other branches, such as Manchester, also used this title for some years. The first ever Samaritan shift outside London took place on 1 June 1959. Though CAL 3333 was scheduled to open officially at 9 am, good publicity ensured that four calls had already been received before the deadline. David Arthur remembers taking the very first call. The caller began by saying,

"Happy birthday, Samaritans", before launching into a catalogue of very serious problems, proving from the outset the need for a branch in Edinburgh. Its first annual report, in 1960, recorded that 550 calls had been received. Those involved as volunteers had, however dropped from around 118 to nearer 50. This was put down to the possibility that the work had proved too exacting for some.

Within a few months there was a cluster of Scottish centres, though not before the first English service outside the capital had been launched in Liverpool. The earliest Scottish operations besides Edinburgh, were in Glasgow, Aberdeen (David Arthur had recently moved there) and Dundee. At that time there was no organisational structure and it was a distinct possibility that the Scottish groups might wish to stay separate from any in England or elsewhere. There were indeed a number of meetings where the possibility was discussed during which David Arthur made the point that whatever was decided should always be for the ultimate benefit of those who wished to use the service. To this day the benefit to the caller is of paramount importance. Chad naturally would have found an independent Scotland unacceptable so it was fortunate that the possibility began to recede once a corporate system had been devised at the Durham conference of 1961. To this day, however, the Scottish branches still have a different constitution from that of any other area, the influence of the Kirk and the concept of presbytery leading to a system where the committee had control of all aspects of branch work under the leadership of the chairman. In other areas branches are led by a director who directly supervises all matters relating to callers or to volunteers while the committee and its chairman deal with the business side of running the service.

The Samaritan movement is unique amongst charities in that the national structure was born out of independent operations working at a local level. It was never intended that any central structure should govern the branches, but rather that the branches should each play an active role in the co-ordination of the service.

This meant that a structure was needed to run things, so the Council of Management was born. The Council and its Executive Committee were given complete authority over the setting up (or closure, though this power has only once been exercised) of branches. A booklet published in 1968 entitled, *The Samaritans, how to run a branch (sic)* explains in detail the role of the Council and how to go about setting up a new branch. It explains that the Council is representative of all branches, thus receiving legitimacy. If every branch is represented directly, there is no question of not taking direction from the

Council. This has always been one of the greatest strengths of the Samaritan movement though there have always been attempts to reduce its size on the grounds that it is unwieldy and therefore ineffectual. A full review of the alternative methods of governing the movement concluded in 1996 that this was indeed the right way of running things, a conclusion endorsed by the Council, but this has not prevented succeeding generations of planners from attempting a radical change. In January 2003, the Council voted comfortably for the *status quo*, proving that its members, in common with many volunteers of longstanding would be very unhappy to see the branch influence on the Council reduced to an indirect one through a small body of elected representatives. The great danger is one which has, for most of its history, been avoided by the Samaritans, that of ambitious or *political* individuals taking power to themselves.

The first Memorandum and Articles of Association incorporating The Samaritans as a *Company limited by guarantee and not having a share capital* in accordance with the various Companies Acts, were instituted at a ceremony in the hall of one of the London Guilds on 11 April 1963. To comply with the law a number of individuals had to be named as *subscribers* and each one's identity had to be confirmed by a named witness. The fifteen subscribers included two bishops (both from the Indian sub-continent), a further four clergymen, a doctor, a solicitor, a headmaster from Hong Kong, three company directors, (one from Ireland and one from India), a stockbroker and a Scot

described as *"a Gentleman"*. Thus right from the start of the wider movement there was an intentional inclusivity, not only in the British Isles and Ireland, but worldwide.

By the time of its incorporation, the Samaritans had grown to eight branches to which new ones were being added every week. The first English branch was in Liverpool. It was set up by the Rev. Christopher Pepys who played an influential role in the early days of Samaritan work. The Liverpool centre was begun on the 1 March 1961 with the telephone number of MARitime 9000 - the nearest possible to that

Christopher Pepys' widow, Elizabeth, opens the new centre at Liverpool, from The Samaritan, *1979*

original one in London. Christopher Pepys had taken up the living of St Nicholas at the Pier Head in Liverpool following a tragedy which had traumatised the whole congregation. It was typical of him that he was able to turn this in a positive direction by suggesting that it would be appropriate if this could become the second Samaritan centre in England. The idea was accepted with enthusiasm by the parochial church council, and members of the parish were recruited. Alan, a founder member, recalls that there were 25 lay members in the first instance. Each was given a number following the alphabetical order of their surnames. Thus Alan, who was one of the very first volunteers and in fact covered the first overnight shift in Liverpool became Alan 25 as his surname began with W. Christopher's move south, to become Bishop of Buckingham, did not prevent him from giving further help and support including the encouragement to set up an administrative office in Slough in the late 60s.

In the early 60s, Chad was in touch with clergy all over the country so that within a short time there were many more branches being set up. The first seven of these were, in order, London, Edinburgh, Liverpool, Glasgow, Stanmore, which disappeared from the scene very soon, Aberdeen and Manchester with Bournemouth and Derby in eighth and ninth places. All the English branches were under the direct auspices of local clergy and, as we shall see, were frequently set up in church premises, but the church connection became less important as the organisation gained momentum.

In the ten years between 1959 and 1969 the number of branches had grown from Edinburgh at number two to Watford, (now South West Herts) at number 107. This rapid expansion brought with it a need to divide branches

Christopher Pepys

into regions. Some of the regional groupings seem rather strange to us since Belfast branch, the first across the Irish Sea and number 13, was designated part of the North West region. It was led for many years by two remarkable men. Bill Thomson was to become the first national chairman after Chad and his successor, Sidney Callaghan, a Methodist minister was a flamboyant character whose *touch of the Blarney* could sway the Council of Management within seconds, as many who remember him will testify. Belfast branch was for nearly ten years on its own until the foundation of Dublin in

1970 as number 110. The Irish Republican situation was quite different from that in England, Scotland and Wales in that the Church, far from being a formative influence, was actively opposed to the work since suicide was considered by Catholics to be a sin and therefore a somewhat taboo subject. In some areas, such as Limerick, there even seem to have been demonstrations in the street against the setting up of branches. It is not surprising therefore that the Dublin branch was set up by a Protestant clergyman, Billy Wynne. It was his patient work, with the support of some enlightened Catholics, which finally convinced the Church authorities that the Samaritan organisation was a good thing. Dublin was rapidly followed by Coleraine and there are now 20 branches in the Irish region.

The most notable feature of this region is its ability to transcend the sectarian divide and retain the respect of all parties in this troubled area. When suggestions have been made that regions should be made smaller, Ireland is always quoted as the reason not to split, since a north/south divide there would be entirely against the spirit of unity which has always existed. The trust and respect given to Samaritans by all sides in the North has meant that one of the less welcome results has been the use of Samaritan lines to transmit bomb warnings. This has sometimes spilled over into mainland Britain where warnings of local bombings have come through on the emergency phones. Some Irish branches, such as Newry, very near to the border, have been directly affected during the height of the troubles. The location of the centre, across the road from the RUC station meant that volunteers were frequently having to sweep up the debris after a bomb attack on their neighbours. Their callers and potential volunteers were often too frightened to visit, but their location made the premises unsaleable. Eventually many branches throughout the movement donated money so that a relocation could be effected.

By 1976 there were 165 branches, and, after a final spurt in the 80s, when a number of branches had associate groups in nearby locations, there are now 203 stretching from Shetland in the north to Guernsey in the south and from Great Yarmouth in the east to Kerry in the west of Ireland. Some of those small groups became full branches while others were deemed to be unviable. Now with modern telephone technology the tendency is not to start any new branches, but rather to consolidate the service which can be offered so that it is consistent both in availability and in quality.

...and wider

The early years of The Samaritans were somewhat paralleled in Europe. In a number of countries similar concerns about suicide were being addressed in the

founding of centres to offer help. As more and more countries became involved, an association, informal at first, began to emerge. At Château de Bossey in 1960 Professor Schwyn recognised Chad's contribution by welcoming him, much to Chad's amazement, as *"Our beloved Founder"*. This association was at first intended to be an information centre but within a short time it had become a federation, the International Federation of Telephonic Emergency Services (IFOTES). In some areas, notably Germany and Sweden the input of local churchmen was inclined to be evangelising, a characteristic viewed with much suspicion by Chad who believed that some parsons could not stop preaching, a far cry from the accepting nature of befriending upon which he insisted. Nevertheless The Samaritans remained a part of IFOTES for 17 years until Chad persuaded the Council of Management that their membership was inappropriate. Membership of other organisations such as IASP, the International Association for Suicide Prevention which has Transatlantic connections as well as European, has continued.

A visitor from Hong Kong in the Manchester centre

In 1970 an overseas committee was set up with Chad in the chair, a sign of Samaritan concerns about possible work in other countries, and in 1974 an important development took place on the worldwide front. Chad set up Befrienders International (BI) which brought together work which was already being done in Hong Kong (since 1963), Rhodesia, (now Zimbabwe) where there were already three centres, Singapore, Australia, New Zealand, where there were two centres, and the Indian sub-continent. These centres, though working in the same way as their British and Irish colleagues, were becoming out of touch because of the distance, so that a more formal structure became desirable. There were funds available, some from the Gulbenkian Foundation, but there was some controversy in the Council of Management over the use of Samaritan funds for the development of BI. This happily did not stop the rapid expansion of branches worldwide. Tireless work by the Founder who regularly travelled thousands of miles to all parts of the world in his quest to set up centres resulted in rapid expansion, so that by the late 1990s there were almost 150 centres working to Samaritan principles, though not necessarily using the same name. The Samaritans became a member of BI and provided the largest

Publicity leaflet for the Cantonese speaking branch in Hong Kong

contingent, 203 branches, but each of the other major areas of the world is represented amongst the membership. In South America there are 49 centres (mainly in Brazil), in North America there are 11, all in New England or New York. There are also four in the West Indies. There are six in the former Soviet Union, two in former Yugoslavia, two in Eastern Europe and 25 in the rest of Europe. In Africa six centres exist plus one in Egypt, and in India there are six, with eight in Sri Lanka. In south east Asia there are nine including one in Japan. Finally in Australasia there are 13 of which the greater number (nine) are in New Zealand. In 1983 Chad handed over the reins to Vanda Scott who, as director general continued his work.

The existence of BI has been of immense value, bringing together cultures and ideas so that there could be a genuine cross-fertilisation. Poorer centres have been helped in practical ways while others have been enriched by meeting their counterparts from elsewhere in the world. The twinning scheme putting individual centres in touch with others in different countries has been very rewarding for all those concerned thanks to major efforts by Loveday Russell of Central London, (now succeeded by Joan Guénault of Lancaster). Loveday's huge energy and great charm were irresistible and one would find oneself promising all kinds of help and hospitality to our overseas colleagues without even realising one was being asked. Sadly Loveday died just as this book was being prepared for publication. She will be much missed.

BI has never had a major financial foundation and, at the time of writing, its affairs, at least as an organisation, are under review. This will not prevent the work in international centres from going on but the future remains to be seen.

Breakfast in Poland 1998. Loveday makes her point to Chad and Alison (youth co-ordinator) after a BI conference

"For God's sake, keep religion out of it"

As we have seen, the name The Samaritans, was not the original intention of the Founder. In fact it was first coined by the press and its religious connotation has sometimes been a problem especially in the light of Chad Varah's often repeated and fervent opinion that *"preachy parsons"* (his phrase) were certainly not what was required. There is an irony in this since the impetus for expansion across the British Isles and Irish Republic came very largely, though not exclusively, from church ministers and their congregations. In fact, despite his injunction, Chad himself insisted in the early days that all those in charge of branches as directors or chairmen should be members of the clergy. In a booklet published by the SPCK in the early 60s he specifies that the *Membership* be confined to the laity, using parsons and doctors only as consultants, while the *Direction* should be in the hands of a clergyman who would be advised as necessary by a medical psychiatrist, the parson being a minister of the established or predominant religion in the area, thus in England he (never *she* in those days) would be Church of England while in Scotland he would be Presbyterian. Chad goes on, *"it is important that the direction shall command the widest support and also be free of any suspicion of seeking to proselytise"*. In some branches, for example Bournemouth, this prescription was even written into the constitution which said that *"the director must be a minister of religion, preferably on the staff of St Peter or St Swithin or one of the churches affiliated to the Bournemouth Council of Churches"* (1963). A look at the membership of the Council of Management in 1966 which had around 30 people representing the movement, reveals that 21 were *Revs*.

At first, too, in London there was a religious aspect to the work.

ALL SAINTS CHURCH, PORTSMOUTH

Service of

Inauguration and Commissioning

of

THE

PORTSMOUTH

SAMARITANS

by

The Lord Bishop of Portsmouth

ON TUESDAY, 19th DECEMBER, 1961,

at 8 p.m.

A core body, known as the *Company of Samaritans* attended a religious service where they were admitted. The form of service contained the following: *"the Company of Samaritans is a fellowship of Christians who in the spirit of the parable of the Good Samaritan offer themselves as agents of the Divine compassion to human beings of any race or creed who are tempted to take their own lives. The fellowship associates itself with men and women who do not fully share the beliefs of the Company, but who are in sympathy with its objectives and desire for humanitarian reasons to give what help they may"*.

This makes it clear that there was never any intention of exclusivity and when the membership expanded the services gradually ceased. As late as 1970, though, some branches still held a Christian service for those volunteers who wished to attend.

In 1964 the Executive Committee which included at the time at least eight clergy, passed a resolution which said, *"the previous distinction between Christian and non-Christian is abolished so that the admission service becomes optional, but is, of course, enormously valued by Christian members."*

Many early volunteers like Rosemary 82 of Luton and Edith 1 of Manchester recall that they were recruited by their own vicars. This seems to have been the main source of volunteers in the early days. In fact in Manchester by 1966 though the director and two of his deputies were Church of England clergy and another was a Methodist minister, there were also two female deputies. This was quite unusual and no woman reached the position of national chairman until Nancy Kerr in 1979. Nancy herself remembers going into the main hall at the Swanwick conference centre and seeing before her *"a sea of black"*. Also amongst the Manchester branch membership were several Jewish people, a number of Catholics, a Swedenborgian and some atheists.

Those who led the movement in those days were, as they would be now, very much aware of the dangers of recruiting people of faith who felt called to proselytise or judge According to John Eldrid any caller seeking Samaritan help would, by definition, be in a very vulnerable state and therefore possibly open to *brainwashing*. Any volunteer should avoid the temptation to play the

A "sea of black" (after E W Forrest)

pseudo-psychiatrist, therapist or counsellor. They should be offering befriending, support, love, and contact with another human being.

Christopher Pepys was typical of the many clergy who found time in their busy schedules to become involved in helping to set up and run services for the desperate people in their areas. *"He always pretended to be a figure of fun. In fact he gave courage and hope to thousands of people and inspired hundreds of Samaritans to do the same for others."* (The Samaritan)

He died in 1974.

The opening of the present Macclesfield centre in 1992. At the back is Rex Cannon, later national publicity officer, who began his Samaritan career here

Matters of principle

Once the organisation had become cohesive, and was beginning to spread not only in Britain and Ireland, but also worldwide, it was clearly essential to have a set of guiding rules which could apply in all conditions and circumstances, but would define both the scope and the limitations of the work. To this end the Founder drafted a list of 20 Principles. These were discussed and refined before being adopted by the Executive Committee in January 1973. A few years later a working party under the leadership of the then vice-chairman, Bob Withers, set about updating and restating these fundamental statements. The results of its work were embodied in the Seven Principles and Seven Practices which still formed the core of Samaritan work until a modernisation in January 2003. With one or two exceptions the basic ideas are common to both the 20 and the seven, but there are some changes of detail. The 20 Principles contained a number of statements about what the organisation was not. Number 12 said that it was *non-medical* but went on to say that a caller might be directed to medical help while 13 stated that it was not *a trained case-work agency*. Next it was not a *social welfare agency*, nor was it a *Christian organisation*. One major difference is to be found in Principle 16 which dealt with anonymity. Volunteers remained known only by their forenames unless *"one of the persons in charge of the branch decides what other information may be given to the client concerned and whether hospitality may be offered by the volunteer in his or her own home"*. This would be entirely forbidden nowadays and continuing befriending in most branches would normally be firmly rooted in the centre. There are volunteers of great experience and longstanding who deplore this change. The concept of befriending has always been firmly embodied in the principles, though in the new thinking the word has been replaced by the phrase *emotional support*. The argument for this change is twofold. On the one hand it has been felt that some members of the public might be misled into expecting more from the service than it can offer such as *friendship*, while on the other it is felt that the theory on which Samaritan help is based should not emphasise the matter of suicide, but rather broaden the appeal so that potential callers will not be put off by the idea that the line is a last resort. Availability, complete confidentiality, anonymity, continued support in appropriate cases are still central, and, perhaps most important of all, the belief that a caller is at all times in charge of his own destiny, and free to break contact at any time remains. One change which distinguished the original 20 principles from the seven

THE 7 PRINCIPLES OF THE SAMARITANS.

1. The primary aim of the Samaritans is to be available at any hour of the day or night to befriend those passing through personal crises and in imminent danger of taking their own life.

2. The Samaritans also seek to alleviate human misery, loneliness, despair and depression by listening to and befriending those who feel that they have no-one else to turn to who would understand and accept them.

3. A caller does not lose the freedom to make his own decisions, including the decision to take his own life, and is free to break contact at any time.

4. The fact that a person has asked the help of the Samaritans, together with everything he has said is completely confidential within the organisation unless permission is freely given by the caller for all or part of such information to be communicated to someone outside the organisation.

5. Samaritan volunteers, in befriending callers, will be guided and actively supported by experienced leaders who will have the advice, when required, of professional consultants.

6. In appropriate cases the caller will also be invited to consider seeking professional help in such fields as medicine and social work, and material help from other agencies.

7. Samaritan volunteers are forbidden to impose their own convictions or to influence callers in regard to politics, philosophy or religion.

principles and practices was the approach to third party calls. In the first, *"the Samaritans do not intrude upon persons who have not sought their help directly"* unless they are told by an identifiable person, of someone who is too ill, old or young to call on their own behalf. The more recent Practice Four says that befriending may be discreetly offered to a person about whom another person may be concerned because they are despairing, depressed or suicidal. In other words, third party calls are now more readily accepted. This has been particularly important in the light of all the work which has now been going on for more than two decades building relationships with professionals and other agencies working with vulnerable groups. If a representative of one of these has worries about one of their clients, they may well be able to help them best by contacting the Samaritan branch and asking the volunteers to contact him or her. Such links have been encouraged through national publicity and through branches reaching out to their local communities.

The recent review of the Samaritan image has resulted in a new (though generally similar) set of statements of *Mission, Vision and Values* for use in work in the community, and there is to be more work done in order to bring the Samaritans into the 21st century. It is to be hoped that the fundamental nature of the work will remain unaltered.

—•—

"Come friendly bombs"

Many generations of Samaritan volunteers have been accustomed to referring to *Slough*, otherwise known as the Samaritan General Office, as if it were the fount of all policy and all organisation. In fact of course the Council of Management and its Executive Committee have for many years been the source of these things. However *Slough* always got the blame and the name will live on in many people's memories despite the move in 2001 to Ewell. The new general office is a very far cry from the first one. In fact in the early days there was no general office at all. When there was only the St Stephen's centre in Walbrook, the administration was either done from there or from the homes of individuals. The first secretary was Daphne Morriss who had worked for Chad. Leslie Kentish ran the financial side, though the amounts involved were very small and the two of them constituted the national system. In 1969, however, a general secretary was appointed to take over some of the running. This was the Rev. Basil Higginson who had already founded and been first director of the Manchester branch. He needed a base and managed to beg rooms at different times in the Harrow branch and at Pinewood vicarage courtesy of Christopher Pepys.

Eventually, after struggling for some time in this way, Chad was able through his many influential contacts, including the Grocers' Company, to raise sufficient funds to purchase a property. This was achieved in 1970 when a suburban semi-detached house at 17, Uxbridge Road, Slough, became the first official general office. It cost £8,000 and was in a somewhat parlous state. There were no carpets and the curtains were shredded into strips.

The new general secretary and his staff, which consisted at that time of Vera Feeney, who was employed fulltime and two part-time helpers, had to work hard to set things up. Vera well remembers the simplicity of those early unsophisticated days. Basil said to her *"You've got a Hoover, haven't you?"* and the next day she

Basil Higginson, founder of Manchester branch in 1961 and first general secretary of The Samaritans from 1967. He established the general office at Slough. "His chief concern was for the clients and the ordinary Samaritans in the ordinary branch for whom he has worked tirelessly." (The Samaritan) *Basil retired in 1975 because of ill-health and died shortly after*

vacuumed while Basil cut the lawn and her young son washed up the cups. The office was eventually given a cord carpet and some shelving in the front room paid for by some special fund-raising. Vera no longer had to balance her work precariously on temporary furniture. She recalls that her first week's wages was a heap of coins piled up on her typewriter. Much of the work was still done in people's houses, especially mailings to be sent out to the branches. The documents were copied on an old-fashioned Banda

17, Uxbridge Road, Slough. Now the home of the local Samaritan branch

machine with stencils, and a part-timer was employed to do this work. She used to bring her dog to work and things must have been chaotic when the bookkeeper also brought two retrievers.

Vera Feeney

Vera Feeney's remarkable career spanned the whole of the 31 years of Samaritan administration from Slough. She retired in 2001, much missed by everyone. Vera knew every branch and its history and had a huge wealth of knowledge about the movement in general. She was responsible for setting up official branch visits and had an encyclopaedic knowledge of the circumstances past and present surrounding any given branch. She also knew her panel of visitors very well and would pair people up to work together with unerring skill.

Soon Basil and Vera were joined in the office by Jean Burt who had been a long-standing volunteer at the Central London branch. As assistant general secretary and later joint general secretary with David Evans, she gave sterling service in the early days of the administration.

Albert Jewell, national chairman 1986 - 1988 remembers what it was like in those days at Slough.

"One of the great eye-openers in those days was to discover that the semi-detached premises at Slough were so small and the staff limited to Jean Burt, David Evans, Vera Feeney as office manager and general factotum, plus one or two secretarial cum clerical workers. Their industry was phenomenal, as was their output - much as the branches may have

deplored all that paper - and all in support of the volunteers who in their turn supported the callers. It was a model of economy and effectiveness."

David Evans, the second general secretary's wisdom and laconic wit helped many a director and chairman over their darkest hours. A raw new director in a flat panic having found out that a former volunteer was about to give the press confidential information was told to be as honest with the press as possible and to point out to them that if they were to print confidential information, it would not damage the Samaritans, but would make the problems of potential callers even worse, since they would feel they had lost a trusted source of help. This sound piece of advice not only helped to avoid a crisis, but helped also to build a very positive relationship with the press in that locality. When he retired from work at the general office in order to take up his role as a Church of England priest again, the then Chairman, Norman Keir wrote the following in The Samaritan:

Jean Burt

When Jean died in March 1990, John Eldrid wrote the following tribute in The Samaritan.

"Jean reflected the special qualities of Christianity and humaneness which enabled her to serve The Samaritans so well, especially in our early days. It was in no small part due to Jean's sense of commitment, sensitivity, fearlessness and intellectual abilities that Chad's great initiative in starting The Samaritans was able to emerge into a worldwide movement for helping the suicidal and despairing."

A worthy epitaph

David Evans

"Perhaps the most concise and accurate description of David is 'the Samaritans' Samaritan'. All those many people who contacted him for advice, found him wholly supportive and ever wise in his counsel. When I think about David, Kipling's poem 'If' always comes to mind, especially the bit about keeping your head when all about you are losing theirs. David is completely unflappable, the ideal companion in a crisis…Those of us who have seen David only at York or Swanwick, national conferences and training schools, will remember him for his shrubbery notices and his splendidly naughty sense of humour."

David was also well known as a railway buff and when he left the office he was presented with a splendid cake in the shape of a train.

When Jean retired as joint general secretary, a new assistant general secretary was appointed. Since 1983 Simon Armson has worked for the Samaritans, eventually taking over as general secretary from David Evans. Latterly, as chief executive, Simon has presided over an enormous increase in the size of the staff and a move out of Slough to the present general office at Ewell.

In a competitive modern world, it is argued, a charity has to make sure that its fund-raising and public relations establishments are comparable with the other major charities. This has led to rapid expansion, so that in 1996 there were 39 staff compared with the 69 reported by the office in October 2002, the majority of whom are relatively new, since many of the long-standing employees felt unable to make the move from Slough. Big business has come to the organisation!

Albert Jewell welcomes HRH the Duchess of Kent to the general office

David Evans with Simon Armson, now the chief executive

The Samaritan magazine

"Where there is much desire to learn, there of necessity will be much arguing, much writing, many opinions; for opinion in good men is but knowledge in the making."

John Milton, *"Areopagitica"*

Any study of the Samaritan movement would not be complete without a dip into the pages of the Samaritan magazine. This small format, unassuming publication has, over the years reflected the full spectrum of Samaritan thinking. Since its first issue in 1972, it has followed all the major debates and issues of burning importance. It continued until recently to present the views, not just of the Council of Management or its Executive, but also of *ordinary* Samaritan volunteers. Without censorship or judgement an opportunity has been provided for sharing views, for reflection and for evaluation. New initiatives have been traced and the opinions, sometimes favourable, sometimes critical, of a wide range of people have been included. Sometimes the articles are wake-up calls to the movement as when in an early issue, No. 15, Anthony from Leicester who became youth officer wrote a swingeing attack on Samaritan complacency and self-righteousness as he saw it at the national conference. Where else could he have delivered his message and provoked so much thought amongst so many people? The tradition of frank discussion has continued. Recent issues have covered some debate on the nature of befriending and the pros and cons of its being *assigned* or not. Other varying points of view have been expressed on issues arising from the *Facing the future* project. Through the pages of the magazine one can trace the evolution of Samaritan thought and most of the major developments which are covered in this book.

As part of the current policy of *rebranding* (2002), the simple unassuming format has become a thing of the past, much mourned by many volunteers. The new, bright, two-tone green *Samaritans' Voice* purports to be its replacement but it remains to be seen whether this new publication can ever live up to its predecessor, for depth, interest and sheer integrity. The question arises whether in 50 years' time the new organ will provide as full and reliable a source of information on the history of the next few years as the Samaritan magazine has been for this volume.

The magazine was edited throughout its history by Elisabeth Salisbury without whose dedication and enthusiasm it could not have succeeded and whose help in producing this work is gratefully acknowledged.

The Samaritans and suicide

From the very first, suicide has been a major focus for Samaritan work. One of the most remarkable aspects of the setting up of the service was that it offered a lifeline (though never exclusively), to two groups of people outside the accepted bounds of society. In 1953 sex and suicide were both taboo, the first because of social mores, the second because of the law. Proffering an accepting and supportive hand to those tormented by sexual problems and those, as the phrase used to be, *tempted to suicide,* was the hallmark of the service, and frequently the two were intertwined. As the work became more widely known the range of difficulties being experienced by those in contact extended, though a major focus continued to be upon suicide.

Once the law had been changed in 1961 by the Suicide Act an unsuccessful suicide could no longer be tried for their attempt, but the stigma still remained. To this day there are many who hide or disguise their suicidal impulses behind a façade of *normal* behaviour because they feel ashamed or guilty about them. Combined with a view that their families and friends would be better off without them, this can lead to a lethal desperation. Permission to share feelings like this can make all the difference between life and death, and this is the premise from which Samaritans work.

The only thing holding her back is a thin piece of cord with you on the end of it.

If you feel you could help people who are at the end of the line, please contact your local Samaritans

the samaritans

Psychiatric and medical supporters of the Samaritans such as Erwin Stengel, Richard Fox and Doris Odlum encouraged the volunteers to be aware of suicidal thoughts, but in the early days the approach was not as it is now. One branch handbook, *Notes for the guidance of members*, issued in 1965 has, under the heading of *General Hints*, a paragraph which reads: *"The person who threatens suicide. It may be a hoax or obviously said to gain attention, but all threats must be taken seriously. Such persons need very firm assurance of help; and firmly told that suicide is no answer to their problem, that it will cause great distress amongst their friends and relatives and is the worst thing they can do...Encourage them to talk about their problems."* Any modern Samaritan volunteer would be horrified by this approach. In the first place the negative suggestion of a hoax is the first point mentioned but beyond this, any idea of telling a caller that suicide is the *worst thing* they can do is diametrically opposed to the modern, better informed way in which help is offered now. A distressed caller already has enough trouble without the volunteer adding guilt to his or her burden. At least the idea of listening, the most important feature of a relationship between a volunteer and a caller was emphasised. Under the heading *Some mistaken opinions*, the points given are: *"that people who talk about suicide won't commit suicide. Around 75% of those who commit suicide have previously attempted or threatened suicide or both. That suicide happens without warning. The suicidal person gives many clues, warnings and indications of his intentions. Alertness and sensitization to these clues will help to prevent suicidal behaviour."* These misapprehensions are still held by many members of the general public and need to be discussed amongst potential volunteers. In the formative years those in the medical and psychiatric professions who helped and advised often emphasised the difference between this type of very personal contact and that between doctor and patient. George Day, a retired GP and expert in psychiatric problems was particularly struck by this when he became a volunteer.

As the movement grew, thinking began to become more focused. The question of the role of Samaritans in suicide prevention began to be looked at in more detail. Involvement and dialogue with many groups and organisations across the world, such as the International Association for Suicide Prevention, (IASP) and The International Federation of Telephonic Emergency Services (IFOTES) for example opened up the debate. Contact with professionals and volunteers all over the world gave new insights into the nature of the work.

By the mid-70s, the issue of suicide became the subject of a new drive within the organisation. It became not only advisable, but essential to ask callers about their suicidal thoughts, feelings and impulses. The idea of asking *the question* was not always received with enthusiasm by local branches. There was still an anxiety amongst some members, commonly shared by the general public, that if the subject was raised, *"it might put the idea into someone's head"*. Experience has shown that not only is this not possible but, on the contrary, a substantial proportion of callers have already been brooding on the subject for a very long time. It is the opening up of the subject which allows the breaching of the floodgates. Nevertheless this mistaken idea has sometimes led to the rejection of Samaritan publicity items. In October 1963 a story appeared in the *Bedford Record* about the refusal of the local bus company to display a Samaritan poster on the grounds that people who travelled regularly in the same seat should not be confronted with the word *suicide* every day.

Dr Roy Vining of the Lowestoft branch whose parallel work on the preparation of volunteers laid the foundations of an inter-active method which was way ahead of its time in the 1970s and early 80s, devised a system for assessing the suicide risk of a caller. This was known for a while by the rather stark title of *lethality scoring.* There were those who felt it was *professionalising* the work and indeed he himself recognised that this might happen. He said, *"for some Samaritans the idea of applying numbers to people will seem repellent, un-British, and un-Samaritan!…but please, even if you don't finish up recording scores, using the table as if you were, will keep the danger signals before your mind, and guide you in what to ask in order to write a true assessment - and, as I hope to show, that can be a matter of life and death."* The lethality score, - *a horrible Americanism*, acknowledged Roy, - did help to enhance the understanding of the nature of suicidal feelings. It looked at such areas as risk factors, for example did the caller live alone? Had there been a bereavement or other loss? This detailed method is no longer used. The risk factors to be identified have been simplified to *suicidal thoughts, active risk* and *suicide in progress.* The understanding gained through its use has now been absorbed into a generally more thorough awareness of the issue which would normally be discussed in preparation classes which all potential volunteers must attend. The notes on how to reach the score were followed by the dictum which still appears on all instructions to volunteers to the present day, *"Ask about suicide at EVERY contact".*

One of the great debates which from time to time rage throughout the Samaritans has been the fundamental question of the Samaritan role in cases where an actual suicide attempt is in progress either during a telephone contact or in a Samaritan centre. In the original Twenty Principles which provided the earliest statement of policy, this topic was covered. In the long accepted Seven Principles and Seven Practices, which provide the basis of the work, Principle Three states, *"A caller does not lose the freedom to make his own decisions, (including the decision to take his own life) and may break contact at any time without fear of being sought out against his will."* At face value this seems simple enough, but on closer examination it reveals a number of important strands. From the early days there had been a school of thought which proclaimed that the volunteer would stay with a caller until he or she died, if that was required. For some this raised the question of what the purpose of the work should be. Suicide prevention as opposed to passive support of a caller came under discussion. There were those who believed that Principle Three meant staying with a dying caller till the end, while others believed that there must be some intervention, at least at the point when the caller became unable, perhaps through unconsciousness, to stay in control. Legal aspects came into play, since the law still considers aiding and abetting a suicide to be a criminal offence. The fact of non-intervention on behalf of a dying caller, in those cases where it would have been possible to get help, could conceivably be taken as *aiding* or *abetting*.

In 1978 at the Council of Management the whole issue was discussed. Doris Odlum, the life president, put her views forward in a characteristically clear and sensible form. She believed that the caller had already abrogated some of the responsibility for his own life simply by asking Samaritans to become involved. The caller must have a purpose in making contact even if he himself was unaware of what it was. In any case the caller would be aware of the Samaritan objective which is to help those who are in despair or suicidal, and obviously this does not mean to help them to die but rather to help them to find it worthwhile to continue living. *"The inference is very strong,"* said Doris, *"that they do in fact wish us to intervene despite what they say."* Her view on one group, however, differed. She believed that someone terminally ill who was shortly to die anyway might legitimately call wanting comfort at the end of their life. This she believed should be given, having checked with the then honorary solicitor, that this would be within the law provided that no action was taken which could conceivably be interpreted as abetting or procuring the suicide.

This part of the debate inevitably became entangled with the related question of euthanasia when, only a year later, the EXIT organisation issued a booklet advising its members how to kill themselves. This prompted a number of calls to Samaritan branches asking for the same information, which was distressing to volunteers and anathema to the organisation, despite the belief in the callers' rights.

The difficulty was such that it prompted Richard Fox, *Hon. Shrink,* to issue a set of guidance notes to all branches, alerting them to the dangers of this document. He emphasised that it would shortly arrive in the public domain in some form, probably pirated, and was very probably illegal as well as being a potential murderer's charter. He went on to discuss advances in terminal care, including the hospice movement, then in its infancy, assuring volunteers that much evidence current at the time showed that many of those who attempted suicide unsuccessfully were eventually glad to be alive.

In the 80s a harder line on the meaning of Principle Three emerged. There were some who believed utterly in the idea of staying with a caller till they died. Although this eventuality hardly ever occurred, it became the subject of much debate over several years until it was finally solved in the early 90s under the chairmanship of Sheila Coggrave. Legal advice given at this time suggested that, despite Samaritan statements of their principles, there was no guarantee that a caller would in fact either know of them or subscribe to them. This could lead to a situation in which a caller might, for example, overdose, then make contact, hoping that some intervention might be made on their behalf. If this did not happen and the caller died, it could lay the Samaritans open to a claim for compensation from the family of the deceased. In 1991 guidelines were issued to branches instructing that if a caller was actually in the process of taking his or her life the volunteer should make it clear that should the caller become unconscious at any stage in the conversation, the volunteer would take action, such as calling an ambulance, if the caller's whereabouts were known. This would give the caller the option of terminating contact should this not be acceptable.

The Samaritan attitude to suicide is summed up by John Eldrid as follows: *"Being involved in helping those who are suicidal constantly reminds us of the despair and sadness of so many people. The outcome of the majority of our encounters will be uncertain, which means we have to cope with our anxieties and to bear with inconclusiveness. We will soon discover, if we have not done so already, how much we have in common with our callers. We will share the deep emotional feelings of love, power, loss, selfishness and weakness as part of our human response. Suicide, like war, can be given romantic, glorious and even honourable descriptions when in reality both are about untimely death and destruction. We should have no illusions about how attractive the solution through death may become to any one of us. It is only when we touch the ultimate that we come, as it were, to the brink and then often we experience inner stirrings of hope.*

The phone kiosk at Beachy Head

Often we will not know the outcome of our meetings yet sometimes, just through even

one intense encounter, the caller's pain will be reduced. Those of us who have had the privilege of seeing many suicidal callers over a large number of years, have learnt from them how much they have been helped. Because of the intensity of our task and the emotional stress of many of our encounters, we need to relax and build up our confidence as an essential part of the helping process. So many people in their desperate hours need to be gently embraced with human warmth, confidence and hope."
(John Eldrid, *Caring for the Suicidal.*)

One of the most notorious places for potential suicides in England is Beachy Head. The Samaritans of Eastbourne campaigned to get the authorities to place a telephone box near to the cliff with a board close by advertising the Samaritan number. Similarly the Clifton suspension bridge in Bristol has a notice at each end.

Samaritan *expertise* in the field of suicide has long been recognised by professionals in the helping services. It has been unique in the fact that it has set a priority on dealing with the whole area of suicidal feelings. Callers have frequently been directed by their other helpers to seek Samaritan support because of their fragile emotional state and the danger of their harming themselves.

Clifton suspension bridge, showing the Samaritan sign

Matters of law

The nature of the work has always meant that Samaritans have had to be aware of legal issues. At the outset, suicide itself was against the law. Someone who did take their own life clearly could not be prosecuted, one who had not succeeded could. This added an extra dimension of pain for those already burdened with despair. It was only in 1961 that the law changed, through the work of many of those who were already, or who were to become supporters of The Samaritans. Tireless letter and article writing by the Founder and the influence of such notables as Doris Odlum and Richard Fox helped to secure the change, though aiding, abetting, assisting or procuring a suicide is to this day illegal.

The Samaritan principles offer both acceptance and total confidentiality to any caller. This has been of enormous importance. Groups whose life-style put them outside the law, and because of this, at risk of blackmail or worse, could share their feelings without fear of reprisal. Before 1966 the rigid laws against homosexuality all too often meant persecution. *Gross indecency* was ferreted out by zealous police and even activity between consenting adults was liable to prosecution. The Samaritans always offered a safe place and there has always been a strong representation of both male and female homosexuals among Samaritan volunteers.

Whilst the organisation has never been in the forefront of campaigning, there is little doubt that its influence has been material in securing changes in the law. The nature of the organisation has always precluded taking a positive stance in a moral or legal arena since this could imply disapproval of the opposite point of view, which is against the Samaritan philosophy of total acceptance. There have however been occasions when pressure groups have endeavoured to enlist its support. When an amendment was proposed to the Abortion Act of 1967 the Select Committee investigating asked The Samaritans for a view. The resultant paper made the principle of confidentiality very clear. The Executive decided that no view should be presented, either for or against. *"They include amongst their numbers people of such diverse moral, theological and political views that they are united only by the common factors of being i) non-judgmental, and non-evangelical in the widest possible sense, ii) dedicated to the help of the distressed person whoever and whatever he or she may be and iii) helping the person by talking the problem out to see a solution to current difficulties. Any volunteer constrained to ventilate to clients particular views on any moral issue...would be...invited to leave."* Some branches were even approached by groups such as *Life* to allow access to training sessions for their workers. This would always be firmly refused since, though many volunteers have strong personal views either for or against issues such as abortion, it is absolutely forbidden to impose them on any caller.

Confidentiality has sometimes come into conflict in the field of law. Principle Four promises absolute confidentiality. This is an issue which intrigues the general public. *"You mean even if the Ripper called, you wouldn't report him?"* This is the kind of question which is asked of speakers. The answer is, of course, that confidentiality cannot be breached even in this extreme situation. This causes consternation, but it is obvious that if confidentiality were to be hedged about with limitations and qualifications, it would fatally compromise the integrity of the work. Not surprisingly the issue has created some problems over the years. What is a branch to do if they are looking after a caller on the premises in pursuit of whose person the police are beating a path to the front door? In this kind of circumstance, recourse might be made to the honorary solicitor. The aim would always be to persuade a caller to give himself up voluntarily. Sometimes a caller may arrive on the doorstep in a state of extreme agitation because of some criminal act he or she has committed. Many years ago a man who had raided a post office and left the postmistress in a pool of blood was finally persuaded that surrender was his only way forward. The fact that volunteers supported him in doing so helped to improve relationships with the local police who accepted that preservation of confidentiality was not to be equated with obstruction.

On one famous occasion the honorary solicitor, Mike Charman, a notable character renowned for his straight talking, went with the then chairman, Nancy Kerr and Jean Burt, the joint general secretary, to see the Chief Constable at New Scotland Yard who was insisting that all crimes confessed to The Samaritans must be reported to the police. According to Mike, a frank discussion sorted out a workable relationship between the two organisations. Nancy recalls that it was a pretty nerve-wracking occasion as Mike turned on his outspoken manner. At least they were following the advice which was generally given to branches - always go as high as you can when dealing with police. Some of the more junior officers sometimes found Samaritan confidentiality a problem. There were occasions when over-zealous officers could try to force co-operation from branches when their superiors were more inclined to accept a kind of *confessional seal* on information regarding callers. Even when the caller was not involved in a crime directly, but had become embroiled in a police case no information could be passed on without permission. On one occasion an officer investigating a murder had been told by a witness that before reporting to the police contact had been made with the local Samaritan branch. He pressed the branch for a verbatim account of the conversation and accused them of obstruction when they were unable to confirm or deny whether the contact had in fact been made or not. In such a case there is no intention of being difficult and, where possible, a way round the problem would be found. In this case the witness was contacted by the branch and asked for permission, in writing, to

Mike Charman

pass on the necessary information. The deadlock was broken and the police officer concerned was pleased to be able to pass the Samaritan telephone number to the widow of the victim, in case she needed support.

There have been a number of occasions over the years when Samaritan volunteers have been called as witnesses in court cases. While this would only happen when there was no danger of breach of confidentiality, it had implications for the anonymity of volunteers. In a court it would be normal for a witness to be announced by full name, but as a volunteer, at least one without a high public profile, such as the director, names were never made public. The way round this was for the magistrate or judge to be asked to take the evidence of identity in writing rather than verbally, which they were usually prepared to do. There were even occasions where the volunteer was allowed to give evidence from behind a screen.

One of the situations in which this kind of problem might arise was in the case of pop festivals, where the Samaritan tent might find itself the target of a drugs bust, but it also happened on occasion at a centre. A caller was on the premises at Central London branch when the police came for him. He had been seen entering the premises. The branch was unable to surrender him or confirm his presence so the police decided to wait on the doorstep. Appeals for the uniformed officers to move away from the entrance made to their superiors were unavailing and the situation became difficult. Then the caller took matters into his own hands by escaping through another route, unbeknown to either volunteers or police.

Nowadays there are several statutory provisions which may mean the police must be admitted; these include the presence on the premises of a person who has committed an arrestable offence or an escaped prisoner. Similarly, the existence of a judge's order, magistrate's warrant or a police order (in terrorist cases) must not be ignored.

A particular hazard in the early days of the Festival branch was the possibility of arrest. In those days there were a number of illegal festivals each year, which were subject to raids, and arrests were made. As the Festival volunteers believed that their presence was as necessary at illegal events as at official ones, it was not unknown for them to find themselves in a black maria on the way to the cells. One volunteer recalls being let off the hook by the intervention of the honorary solicitor who said to her as she left the station *"where are you going now?" "Back to the festival, of course, where we're needed." "Good girl!"* was the reply.

The Samaritans and the medical profession

From the earliest time the Samaritan organisation has been very fortunate in its relationship with members of the medical, and, more particularly, the psychiatric professions. The support and encouragement of notable psychiatrists such as Christine Hamilton, Richard Fox, who for many years described himself as *"The Hon. Shrink"* and his successors, Richard Finlayson and Jim Birley was enormously valuable in convincing their fellow-professionals of the value of Samaritan befriending. These distinguished members of the psychiatric profession not only acted as advocates of the Samaritan method but gave their experience and expertise freely to help with the formulation of policy and the support of volunteers. Richard Fox, for example was the first to suggest the use of inter-active workshop methods in Samaritan training sessions, which came to replace the lecture style which had been used in the early days. This idea was developed by another doctor, Roy Vining whose work on preparation and on identifying suicide risk is covered elsewhere.

This is not to say that there has never been any difficulty in convincing doctors or psychiatrists of the efficacy of the Samaritan method of *befriending*. In the first few decades of the 20th century there was a very different attitude to psychological difficulties and the whole area of mental illness. Psychiatry was after all a fairly new science and the whole area of diagnosis and treatment was only just being developed. George Day, a Norfolk GP and psychiatric consultant, later to be a tower of strength as an active volunteer and member of the Samaritan Executive, began his career as a GP in 1928. He is on record as saying that in those days he had never heard of depressive illness and was therefore inclined to dismiss those suffering from feeling wretched as neurotic or neurasthenic (a word no longer in use) or having a chronic anxiety state. Any patient unfortunate enough to have delusions or to manifest bizarre behaviour was merely locked away for his or her own safety. Even those who were found dead in the local river, he was unable to recognise as suicides who might have been suffering from depressive illness. At that time, in any case, attitudes to suicide encouraged kindly coroners to deliver verdicts of *accidental death* where possible. Later when working in a private TB sanatorium he still, by his own admission, did not recognise depressive illness. After the war things had begun to change. More forms of medication were available. Tranquillisers and sleeping pills were supplementing electro-convulsive therapy (and incidentally providing new means of ending a tormented life). By this time, depressive illness was recognised though its causes were not to be identified till much later. Now, George Day was inclined to over-use this diagnosis, lumping together a whole range of symptoms and treating his patients accordingly. It was only in the 50s and 60s that he began to ponder on the real nature of psychiatric illnesses. He made an important distinction between different types of depression: that caused by a chemical imbalance in the brain *("anyone who has awakened with a king-size hangover the morning after the night before will know how touchy the brain is to noxious fluids")* and that caused by a reaction to some deep feelings or external events. The latter type, referred to by some psychiatrists as *reactive* as opposed to the other, *endogenous* type, George liked to call *dispiritment*. This description fits very well with the kind of feelings described by many Samaritan *clients,* as he would have called them, though his colleagues in the movement never really adopted it as Samaritan terminology. His description of his attitudes and their development over a long career may well reflect the modesty of the man, but it could almost certainly represent the views of many members of the medical professions. He is on record as saying *"had The Samaritans existed then, I should have thought members of my flock were consorting with a gaggle of middle-aged female busybodies, presided over by a beaming clergyman"*.

Sadly there are to this day many members of the general public who believe much the same about those who volunteer their services, though the medical professions on the whole have a much more positive view. Changes in attitude owe much to the work of people like George Day who became one of the most articulate and evangelising of the leading Samaritans of the 60s and 70s, writing many articles for medical and psychiatric journals and addressing Samaritan training schools, conferences, preliminary meetings to encourage local people to go ahead with setting up centres, as well as offering support to those who were in positions of responsibility. His small booklet, *What a young director should know, by one who didn't* was a treasury of wise and witty information for many generations of branch directors and chairmen (in Scotland).

George Day, inseparable from his beloved pipe

While this was being prepared for publication he was anxious to disclaim any godlike authority, saying *"neither Slough nor the Executive*

39

should be suspected of promulgating some of my controversial views". It should perhaps be mentioned that his wit could be acerbic. One volunteer who knew him well called him, *"acetic acid wrapped in pink icing"*. It perhaps did not do to get on his wrong side, but if one was in favour one could expect great kindness. Norman Keir who was chairman towards the end of George's life recalls receiving, quite unsolicited through the post a parcel containing a bottle of his favourite tipple, (Norman being a good Scot it is easy to guess what!). George had a habit of giving his favourite people nick-names such as *Bog-rat* and once booked Norman and his wife into a hotel under the titles of *Sir* and *Lady*.

George died at the age of 89 just as a revised edition of the booklet was going to press in 1989. His wisdom and humour were much missed by those who had worked with him.

George frequently spoke at conferences and to individual branches. The following extract is taken from his talk to a preliminary meeting convened by Monica Dickens, setting up a branch in Boston, Mass:

"What is it like to be a Samaritan? I can tell you. You see I had been retired some months when I became aware that Satan had been viewing my idle hands with anticipatory gusto…

So I applied…with assumed meekness I attended the preparation classes much as an indulgent bishop might refresh himself at a confirmation class run by a curate. But I was soon dumb-founded. Goggle-eyed, I learnt things about the human condition which hitherto had been an unopened book. Shameful to relate I first became acquainted with the reality of endogenous depression. I had always thought vaguely that all despondencies were reactive to some extrinsic cause, albeit lost sometimes to conscious memory. I had my nose well and truly rubbed into all the sexual deviations, none of which I had ever encountered - or if I had I had evidently turned a blind eye and defensively changed the conversation.

I was also trained to answer the phone graciously, to sustain lengthy and unhurried conversations, and to tolerate long silences.

…feeling quite sick with apprehension…I did my first 3¹/2 hours manning the centre (a tumbledown cottage in a back street). A new client timidly presented herself at the front door…I found myself in a unique situation: the opportunity to give undivided attention and unlimited time to someone in distress…With very little prompting she poured out her troubles. Her problem appeared insoluble…From being tense, agitated and weepy, with more than a hint of suicidal desperation, she gradually calmed down, relaxed and revived.

It was like witnessing the bursting of an abscess… I had done nothing…but thoughtfully grunt, throw in the odd question for elucidation…given no advice…expressed no personal opinion…At the end she rose, and said 'I feel so much better for having talked to you…You have made me feel worthwhile.'…Her life situation was unchanged but she came to accept and live with it."

He was always keen to emphasise the *non-professional* nature of the work, in the most positive terms:

"more than 98% of our field workers are ordinary everyday people, amateurs in every sense of the word. They have no professional qualifications…the professionals, doctors, priests, psychiatrists - still remain, as it were, in the inner sanctum, available for consultation when occasion arises…Neither a clergyman nor a doctor with a stethoscope round his neck can enter this essential relationship with a client. I know this from my personal experience. Whenever it leaks out to a client that I once practised medicine, or worse, psychiatry, I am sunk. No longer are my feet on the same strip of carpet."

The debate about how professional the Samaritans should be raged for many years and raised quite strong passions. Some believed that the word should never be used in connection with Samaritan work while others, who could be said to have prevailed in the end, believed that one could work in a thoroughly *professional* manner, that is, effectively and consistently, without losing the central ethos, that of volunteers being *ordinary people.*

A remarkable lady

Doris Odlum, MA, MRCS, LRCP, DPM.
1890-1985

Over the years the Samaritan movement has been privileged to be associated with some remarkable people. None could be more outstanding than Doris Odlum. In 1961 when Chad Varah first approached her to become psychiatric consultant to The Samaritans she already had a life's work, impressive by all kinds of standard, behind her. After taking a degree in classics, she changed direction entirely to become a qualified psychiatrist in 1924. At that time these professionals were known as *alienists*, a title which Doris actively worked to change, being a member of the British Medical Association which coined the word *psychiatrist* in 1934. As she herself said, patients were *"not aliens, but ill"*.

In 1960 she was a member of the Doctors' and Magistrates' Committee of the BMA whose remit to look at the law regarding suicide led to the repeal of the Suicide Act in 1961, making an attempt to kill oneself no longer a crime. It was her report on this issue which made Chad ask her to become involved.

As a professional she was initially somewhat concerned about the possibility that Samaritan volunteers might either become *pseudo-psychologists* or allow themselves to become emotionally involved with their clients, but she soon became convinced of the efficacy of the Samaritan method.

For the next 25 years, Doris worked tirelessly

"Parents should not press their young sons into being too manly, a woman psychiatrist warns today.

For the result can be just the opposite of what they want, says 85-year-old Dr Doris Odlum. A boy who fails to come up to expectations may become timid and insecure.

Sensitive ones could have their normal development seriously hampered and find it difficult for the rest of their lives to form happy relationships.

Dr Odlum, a leading member of MIND, the national association for mental health, and President of The Samaritans gives her advice in a booklet, *Understanding your child - the first five years*....The boy is required above all things to be a man. The denial of all forms of fear or anxiety or any other emotion can place him under severe strain from babyhood onwards."

Daily Mail, February 1976

in every area of the work, becoming actively involved in her local branch, Bournemouth, which was one of the eight earliest to be founded. Her published work both within the organisation and in publicising the work outside was prolific and full of great wisdom and common sense. As consultant and member of the Executive Committee and from 1968 as honorary life president, the only one ever appointed, she was always to be seen at Council meetings, training schools at Swanwick and at national conferences where she could be relied upon to share her wise thoughts on any issues of concern. Her very last speech to the national conference was delivered, as always, in a clear and comprehensible fashion. She was by that time suffering badly from angina, but no-one in the audience would have had the slightest inkling of her state of health. In her speech she exhorted those present to *"Keep this vision, keep the line, for this way we can give people the most help. Nothing is so dangerous as success, it loses the drive, it loses the original ideas. People put pressure on us to try new things. We are sticking with our original principles."*... She died only three weeks later at the great age of 95.

The following extract, from *Psychological problems and the role of The Samaritans* illustrates exactly her down-to-earth style of encouragement:

"We need to be more flexible in our approach, avoiding labels..: as far as humanly possible...We must realise and accept the fact that we shall have failures. The conscientious type of person, and undoubtedly all Samaritans are of this type, can be extremely discouraged if they fail... The right attitude is to think I did my best...

Perhaps the greatest service a Samaritan can give is to be a good listener. The value of just listening to a person without interruption or criticism cannot be over-estimated.

There is healing in just being listened to...Indeed if the Samaritans were ever to adopt an emblem, it might well be the sign of the listening ear."

It was not till a number of years after her death that a new publicity item appeared. She would have been delighted.

Doris' prolific output of books, articles and pamphlets, both produced for Samaritan use and for raising awareness about suicidal behaviour and a wide variety of psychological difficulties, was tremendously influential in the development of Samaritan thought. In the days when some volunteers were still

Open 24 hours a day.

admitted to the work without any real formal training her ideas were readily available, offering reassurance and support to the unconfident.

In the early days, the methods and approaches to distressed callers still varied somewhat. There was no formal injunction, as there is now, to explore the suicidal thoughts, feelings and impulses of those who called. This was only formalised in the 1970s, though there had been a general encouragement to do so before this, at least with some caution.

It was the work of thinkers like Doris which enabled great changes to come about. Inside the movement she worked on a variety of issues, contributing as consultant or as a member of various working parties to discussion and investigation of, amongst many other areas, the impact of sex calls on branches.

Another discussion, central to the work of the Samaritans to which Doris made a considerable contribution, was how to deal with a caller who was actually in the process of taking his or her own life. Her ideas helped to clarify this very difficult area. She was not only interested in the topics which directly involved her specialism however, joining in the debate on the structure of the movement which was first raised in the late 1970s.

Her output of work in the public sector covered a huge range of material on the various stages of human development. Her studies on childhood and adolescence, the development of the male psyche and many others gained recognition in her own profession and coverage in the newspapers.

Samaritan volunteers were extremely lucky to have the benefit of much of her thinking, not only through her addresses to conferences and training schools but also through a comprehensive series of articles in the Samaritan magazine and several booklets specially written to help volunteers with their work.

Her book *Adolescence* published by Wayland in 1957 sold hundreds of thousands of copies containing, as it does, advice on how to work with adolescents. Mischievously in the introduction, she suggests that people who deny that they had any difficulty at that stage of their development seem to have learnt nothing from these years. *"Such people are almost always afraid of adolescents and are therefore hostile to them."* She suggests that in order to get the best out of the book, the reader should try to think and feel him or herself back into the experience of adolescence, coming in the end to assess what those years meant, what was learnt and how they can be used to help others in dealing with their problems of adolescence. To Samaritans she said, *"It is necessary for us to try and think back and feel ourselves as far as we can into their situation and their emotional reactions. Because we have reached the parental stage of development, we find it extremely difficult not to adopt this attitude. In nearly every case the relations between parents and the child are important factors in the problem. It is essential that we try to rid ourselves of the tendency. If we fail in this, we shall merely give the child the impression that we are being governessy and authoritarian and that we shall side with their parents against them." (Helping children and adolescents, the Samaritan approach, 1974.)*

It is easy to see why Doris and Samaritans were so compatible.

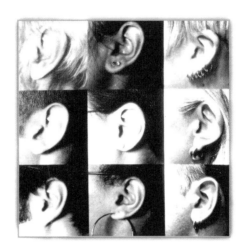

Sex and The Samaritans

In this sexually liberated, outspoken (some may say over-permissive) society, at the start of the 21st century, when absolutely anything goes, it is hard to imagine the social mores and attitudes to all sexual matters of the immediate post-war period. In those days it was shameful to be born *a bastard* while nowadays a large proportion of children born have unmarried parents. Such *social deviants* as unmarried mothers were treated with scorn by some and with kindly, though patronising, paternalism by others. If a young woman found herself pregnant she was often either hidden away until the child was born or ostracised by her neighbours. Young men might sow their wild oats but girls absolutely did not. Churches employed *moral welfare workers* who ran mother and baby homes, and worked with the mothers. In many cases the child was taken for adoption, not always with the mother's informed consent.

There was a great deal of sexual ignorance. Girls were sometimes told nothing of what to expect on their wedding night, an attitude encapsulated in the admonition of the previous century, (whether real or apocryphal) to *"lie back and think of England"*. Sometimes even the young men were left in ignorance of the mechanics of a sexual relationship as a recent television programme showed, so that some marriages were never consummated. Though the problem may rarely have been as extreme, it certainly happened. Anxieties about unwanted pregnancy or sexual difficulties in a relationship could often lead to seriously suicidal thoughts.

Perhaps even harder to bear were difficulties concerning sexual orientation. This was particularly problematic since male homosexuality (though not lesbianism, which, the story goes, was exempted from the law as Queen Victoria could not believe it ever happened), was actually illegal, even between consenting adults. Not only might a man feel guilty because of his feelings but his whole life could be destroyed by a lurid court case or by blackmail. Even worse, he could not dare to share his feelings with anyone. Issues of gender dysphoria and tranvestism were similarly taboo. No gender re-assignment operations were allowed in Britain and it was necessary to travel to somewhere like Tangier to get the operation. One tragic client befriended by a branch in the 60s had tried to emasculate himself by using a grease gun to inject his testicles hoping that they would drop off.

For those with sexual anxieties, The Samaritans provided a safe haven, a warm and confidential place where their deepest feelings could be aired. In the early days a high proportion of those seeking help were suffering because of sex. Chad has always been renowned for his uncompromising attitude to inhibited or shockable volunteers. His emphasis on being non-judgmental meant that there was no room for narrow-mindedness. At an initial meeting of potential volunteers in Cardiff in the early 60s, according to Sue, 140 people turned up but in the second week after one of Chad's colourful talks on sex, only 70 came. At Cambridge in similar circumstances a lady was heard to remark, *"I didn't think such things had happened since ancient Greece!"*. In an account of the Bedford branch, the author, Fred, remembers a time around 1969 when *the cosy serenity* of the branch was shattered by a talk from a Samaritan from London branch who gave a talk on sexual behaviour *"with such brutal frankness that most of the audience hit the roof"*. It is alleged that the ulterior motive for this talk was to smash *the twinset and pearls* image of the branch. *"We had probably not been so shocked since Chad Varah's visit"* (in 1963), remembers Fred. Some, such as those in areas of Britain where religion had a particularly strong influence, did not like Chad because he talked about sex. In some cases male volunteers were very protective of female volunteers who seemed to be being exploited by explicit calls from male callers. This was so extreme in the early days that in one case (the branch shall remain nameless) the male volunteer on duty was so incensed that he traced the call and rushed round in person to the phone box and pulled the offending caller unceremoniously out of it! Nowadays, it must be emphasised, that such an action would not be possible as no calls can be traced since all confidential lines are excluded from the 1471 facility, and no volunteer would dream of behaving like this. In fact many a volunteer who had been brought up in a traditional *respectable* fashion would confess to having learned a great deal from their Samaritan work, much of it quite extraordinary. For Chad one of the issues of great concern was masturbation. There had always been a burden of guilt laid on young men but he realised that sometimes it could be a symptom of deep-seated feelings of inadequacy and isolation. Some of those he tried to help proved to be seriously and suicidally depressed. He believed that if befriended in a particular structured way these men could be helped to overcome their despair. His interest in the matter attracted the label *Dirty old man* to Chad who, far from being discouraged, gloried in it, and in 1973 set about organising the system which used a telephone line which had, in the past, been dedicated to taking calls from the Brent branch so that the line became known as *the Brent line* and subsequently *the Brenda line*. Brenda volunteers were specially selected and trained for this work.

When the tabloid press got hold of the story, they made hay, as they had on previous occasions. A screaming headline in the *News of the World* in August 1974 read *"Smutty callers jam the lifelines"*. In fact the understanding of many journalists as to what it was all about was seriously flawed. The careful structure and monitoring was intended to prevent callers from simply using it as a means to obtain sexual gratification. Interestingly no-one in our present age would turn a hair, given the proliferation of chat-lines and explicit web-sites.

Many Brenda volunteers are convinced to this day that the service did help some callers. The changes in social attitudes and behaviours have reduced the need for such a scheme, though Chad would disagree.

Sexually demanding callers have been an issue within the organisation for many years and one which has sometimes become clouded by a number of issues. Samaritans claim not to judge their callers, yet for some any lack of acceptance of a masturbating caller might be seen precisely in this light. On the other hand, the Founder himself and many of the great thinkers and professional advisors have reiterated time and again that there are some callers who cannot be helped. For these callers there is no solution because they can never get enough of what they want. An exclusively sexually demanding caller is not able to move on from his position which may be entrenched and obsessive. No volunteer entering into a fantasy world with such a caller is going to be able to help, only reinforce the existing pattern. Having said this, there are two caveats. Firstly volunteers are instructed always to investigate the caller's possible suicidal thoughts. Many of them are desperately unhappy and isolated. Offers to discuss these feelings should always be made, though if the caller is unable or unwilling to respond the volunteer may eventually, and as sensitively as possible, end the call. The second caveat is that sometimes a caller's approach may give the impression that he (it usually is *he*) falls into the unhelpable group whereas in fact his problem is a very real one in the area of sexuality or sexual behaviour. In this case a Samaritan listening ear may well be helpful.

How to run a Brenda service.

1. Callers would be carefully selected to include only those thought to be capable of benefiting from the system.

2. Selection of those callers would only be made after a number of contacts.

3. Each caller would have a code-name which had a male and a female part. Thus a caller might give his name as "Tom for Ann".

4. Regular meetings would be held to discuss caller progress and offer volunteer support.

5. Callers who were considered to be abusing the system by satisfying their sexual needs without accepting other help would be banned from it.

6. No uncoded caller would be allowed to masturbate during a phone call.

In 1971 at a national conference a meeting of female Samaritans was held, chaired by the national president, Dr Doris Odlum. This was the first time that a general discussion of the topic was held from which new thinking began to emerge. In 1976 Doris chaired a working party which was set up to discuss the impact of sex calls on branches and volunteers, which she felt needed to be investigated as this type of call appeared to be placing a strain on the resources of many branches. In 1977 she wrote, *"I am interested in their sense of helplessness and their doubt if they are really helping the client in the long run, or even fear that they may be aggravating his problem."*

Sadly without the blessing of the Founder, who felt that many genuinely suffering men were being rejected by the volunteers, a set of guidelines was eventually drawn up which helped to lift some of the burden from volunteers who had sometimes found their whole shifts taken up with demanding and apparently unhelpable men, leaving the question of how many callers who might have been helped were not able to make contact because of blocked lines.

In fact branches who began to monitor their sexually demanding callers closely were amazed to find that what seemed to be a large number could be whittled down to perhaps eight or nine, repeating calls frequently but using different names. Clues of mannerism, turn of phrase and content of calls gave the game away so that volunteers could challenge the caller by saying something like, *"haven't we spoken before? I think you told me…"*. This kind of challenge could persuade the caller to ring off.

Cartoon reprinted from The Samaritan
*where it was reproduced by kind permission
of* Private Eye

Alarums and excursions: dramas and disasters

According to one very long-standing volunteer the situation in the early days was like *"the blind leading the blind"*. She believes that listening skills, now so central to the befriending method, were not really valued then. *"We were doers rather than listeners,"* she says, adding *"now we've gone too far the other way"*.

Early volunteers can tell hair-raising tales about their experiences. It was not uncommon to be excused from the shift in the centre (leaving a solitary volunteer in charge) in order to rescue some very distressed caller (then known as clients) from a desperate situation. A battered woman in a rundown housing estate rang to say that she and her baby were desperate to leave her abusing partner. He was out of the house at present. Could Samaritans help? The baby clinched the matter and one of the shift was despatched to see what could be done. Meeting another volunteer from the *flying squad* en route, the intrepid pair ventured into the house. A sight of indescribable deprivation and squalor met them. There was little in the way of furniture, no carpets and a grate full, not of fire, but of empty cigarette cartons. In the next room the only piece of furniture was a cot in which, swathed in urine-soaked bedding, was an infant. The urgency of the situation became apparent when the client warned the volunteers that the partner was due back any moment. Mother and child were whisked away to the centre - just in time to avoid the man who was a few yards away down the road.

It was not unusual for volunteers to be called out in the middle of the night, or even during the day, sometimes at great risk to life and limb. Nowadays it would not be imagined that two lady volunteers should be wandering around Manchester's Moss Side district looking for a caller who was cutting herself at three in the morning, yet in the early days this kind of thing was not infrequent. Many can tell tales of knives being drawn or guns waved. Picture a quiet Sunday morning, a very suicidal caller arriving on the doorstep of the Samaritan centre in a highly volatile and distressed condition. One of the volunteers, after getting permission from the director on duty put her in the car and set off for the local hospital. Half a mile on the caller pulled out a 10-inch carving knife. Not missing a breath the volunteer asked what the blade was for. *"Oh not for you, it's for me."* With a little persuasion the knife was surrendered and the trip to the hospital completed. The car driver found the weapon under the car seat six months later! Dale of Worthing remembered a *flying squad* call he once took. Writing in the Samaritan magazine in Spring 1978 he describes finding his caller, somewhat the worse for drink in a telephone box. At first the man was highly suspicious but was persuaded to join the volunteer in his car. As he got in, he hit his head on the rim of  the car roof but refused any help to deal with the trickle of blood which ran down his temple. His would-be helper then tried to make him comfortable by closing the door, only to find that his left leg was still dangling outside. As the volunteer tried to redeem this inauspicious start, the client said, *"it would have been a bloody sight less painful if you had let me kill myself!"*.

A founder member from Tunbridge Wells remembers talking to a client in a car at a remote spot on his own with a shot-gun at the ready. It belonged to the client of course.

Reg from Bournemouth remembered for their 40th anniversary booklet, an incident which almost finished his Samaritan career. He was covering the overnight calls when an urgent message came that a very suicidal man was trying to throw himself off the cliff. Finding none of the usual emergency volunteers available, he went out himself and found the client holding a large bottle of aspirins which he was swallowing at intervals. Not knowing quite how to proceed Reg said, *"aren't you going to offer me one?"* to which the caller replied, *"these are not sweets but I have some Polos in my pocket. Would you like one?"*. As he struggled to get the mints out, Reg was able to relieve him of the pill bottle. A little later, when the two had got into the volunteer's car, the caller produced a sharp vegetable knife, with which to slit his wrists. Having been persuaded not to use the knife in what was, in fact, a new car, the caller began to talk. Reg surreptitiously purloined the knife and put it out of harm's way. Eventually he left the man, now calmer, with the excuse that he needed to phone his wife. He actually phoned the director, Eric, who came at once to his aid. They took the caller back to the rectory and Eric took over for a while discussing, as he later reported, philosophy in depth with the *highly intelligent* client. By this time it was morning and Reg staggered home emotionally and physically exhausted, saying to himself that this was the end of his Samaritan career. Later, Eric told him, *"that man said to me, 'Padre, if a complete stranger will*

National Executive 1985

This picture shows many of those who have contributed much to the Samaritan movement. Nat Smith, Albert Jewell, Norman Keir, all former chairmen; Norman Whiting and Joan Guénault, training co-ordinators; Rex Cannon, publicity officer; Jim Birley, hon. psychiatrist; Mike Charman, hon. solicitor; Loveday Russell and Liz Reeve, Maurice Walton of Northampton - vice-chairs and all the regional representatives

In
DISTRESS
or
DESPAIR
ring
SAMARITANS
Phone :
MANSION HOUSE **9000**

HRH the Duchess of Kent launches the single number

Ben Finny, (right) the first co-ordinator for work with older people with her team and her successor. Second from right is Rex Cannon noted for his work in the publicity field and his association with Festival branch. Centre, seated, is Elisabeth Salisbury (Reading and now Oxford), the talented and much respected editor of the Samaritan magazine, from its inception till 2002. Also pictured from the left are Hilary from Manchester, Derek from Leatherhead and Nancy from Hamilton

The Founder at York with Sheila Coggrave, 1993

Loveday, Sheila and Vera with the author at a BI conference in Olsztyn, Poland, 1998

Volunteers at Madras

The chairmen of Samaritans 2002. From the left; John Eldrid, John Lawrie, Nancy Kerr, Nat Smith, Norman Keir, Jenny Cunnington, Sheila Coggrave, David Arthur

The author with the Founder at York, 2000

NW region directors at Whalley Abbey before the regional boundaries meant the loss of Carlisle, Whitehaven, Chester, Rhyl and Bangor (North Wales)

The mobile promotion unit

Samaritans' patron, HRH the Prince of Wales

Stockport volunteers clean up their near-derelict centre before opening, 1979

Arnold helping to launch a major fund-raising drive. Norah his "mum", Albert Jewell and David Evans are in attendance

Arnold's birthday cake

A major fund-raiser

8000 contacted Samaritans last year

NEARLY 8000 people got in touch with the Bangor and North Down branch of the Samaritans last year.

This was just one of the facts revealed during last week's annual general meeting of the local branch in the Winston Hotel.

It was just over two years ago that the local branch of the Samaritans found themselves in dire financial circumstances and at one point faced closure but, according to Betty, Director of the Dufferin Avenue based branch, donations from the public has enabled the work of the Samaritan volunteers to continue today.

She said: "We owe a debt of gratitude to the many supporters inside and outside the Branch who are the means by which it remains open. Time is given freely by volunteers but at a high personal cost to maintain a regular, reliable commitment and ensure 24 hour service to callers."

During the meeting, which was also addressed by principal Social Worker for South and East Belfast Marion Gibson, Betty explained that it cost 140 a day to keep the premises at 90 Dufferin Avenue open 24 hours a day. However the money which had to be spent each day was worth every penny because of the unique service the Samaritans offer: "What is it we have and can offer that other agencies do not? We have a human face and voice with which contact can be made during a 24 hour period. No answering phone greets our callers and no appointment systems defers them for two or three weeks. The financial statement shows figures but our assets are volunteers who were there for the 7676 callers who needed us last year," she said.

Concluding her report Betty invited members of the public interested in working for the Samaritans to come along to their preparation class on October 8.

Pictured at the annual general meeting of the Bangor and North Down Branch of the Samaritans are Marion Gibson, Principal Social Worker for South and East Belfast, Betty, director of the local branch and volunteer Marianne who is the branch chairman.

Centre Page
Daily Mail
27·10·60
PAGE 13

EVERY TIME THEIR PHONE RINGS, SOMEONE SAYS:

I'LL KILL MYSELF!

Sheena Oliver meets folk who keep a vigil for the desperate

FAR and NEAR

Dial D for 'Don't do it'

COMEDIAN Jimmy Logan appealed in Glasgow last night for 120 volunteers to join the Telephone Samaritans, who try to prevent suicides.

In Glasgow last year there were 107 suicides and 24 attempts. Launching the appeal, Jimmy said a round-the-clock service at DOU 4444 was the aim.

● Jimmy Logan signs autographs after opening the Telephone Samaritan Service Coffee Morning in the Glasgow City Chambers to-day.

SIGN ON THE DOTTED LINE.

...TO BE A GOOD SAMARITAN

AN appeal for 120 voluntary workers to join the Glasgow branch of the Telephone Samaritan Service was launched by Jimmy Logan at a coffee morning in Glasgow.

Referring to the 107 suicide cases in Glasgow last year, Jimmy told an audience of about 200 people who die that way would not have taken the step.

The number of attempted suicides in Glasgow last year was 131.

Said the chairman of the service, the Rev. A. Scott Donald: "We have dealt with 100 cases since we started in May of this year."

People who are thinking of taking their own lives are encouraged to dial DOU-GLAS 4444, where we have 70 volunteers ready to listen to their worries. But we need at least other 120 volunteers to enable us to run a round-the-clock service."

EVENING TIMES
24·10·60

Woman's Own   19th June 1961

MONICA DICKENS

Dial M to end despair

Day and night, the Rev. Chad Varah waits to give new hope to men and women who feel life holds nothing more for them.

IN the fourth volume of the London telephone directory there is an entry which says, simply: "Suicide (The Samaritans). The number is MANSION House 9000. It is a number which spells hope, courage, the promise that nothing is ever quite as bad as it seems.

In the last seven years it has meant, quite literally, the difference between life and death for thousands of men and women.

Anyone may call this number at any time of the day or night. There is always someone there to answer. Someone to say that there is no problem so shocking, no mistake so terrible that it can be ended only in death.

would apply for the living of the church, the Rev. Chad Varah.

That was the first miracle. The next thing was to get a telephone number that people would easily remember. The initial contact in his crusade against despair had to be something that required that least effort—less effort than turning on the gas or swallowing the bottle of sleeping pills.

Work in the church was not yet finished, and the telephone was half buried under a pile of lumber. Digging it out, he found that it still worked, and called the telephone office to ask if he could have the number MANSION House 9000. Possibly, they said, if it was not already in use. "What number are you smoking already in use...

from now?"

When he wiped the dust off the face of the dial, the number he uncovered was MAN 9000. It was just one of the countless little things that were piling him his idea was right. Things that seem people might call luck, or coincidence. But things that he called miracles, the sort of miracles that have been happening all the time since he started the Samaritans as a one-man service.

Tuesday, January 16, 1962   EVENING TIMES   Page 5

Vincent Donnelly

LOOKING AROUND

THE English and Welsh are more inclined to suicide than the Scots, says the latest international health report.

The suicide rate per 100,000 people in England and Wales is 11.5. In Scotland it is only 8.5.

Yesterday I talked to some of the people who help to keep the Scottish rate so low—the voluntary workers behind the Telephone Samaritans service in Glasgow.

Suicide call

Would-be suicides sign dou Douglas 4444 at any hour of the day or night. During the day incoming calls re handled by a team drawn from 90 'Samaritans' after dark a minister keeps an all-night vigil by the telephone.

The necessity of the service told

Cuttings submitted by Alice of Glasgow and others

Counting the pennies in Bangor, North Down

The 21st-century logo on display: Christmas stall 2002, Jean and Karen of Manchester

spend all night with me, I am prepared to give you a chance.' You were able to establish a rapport with him. Don't you think you should use that talent?" This kept him in the work for many years to come.

In Liverpool the branch had use of the vehicle belonging to the parish in whose premises it was based. This allowed plenty of rushing round the city *rescuing* people. Sometimes the volunteers themselves needed rescuing as in the case of the curate who found himself cowering beside a terrified wife and children who were trying to hide from a knife being wielded by a raging, unbalanced husband. In a similar case, the two volunteers who had been sent to help found themselves on the receiving end of a hail of crockery being hurled by a hysterical wife at her husband and children. Another volunteer was taken for the *other woman* and found herself threatened by the deserted wife's father.

Another volunteer was sent out in the middle of the night to find a very suicidal caller whose telephone conversation from a call box had suddenly been

Just call me "X"

cut off. He was stopped by a police patrol who saw him listening at phone box doors and assumed he must be up to no good.

It was also possible to get into other kinds of trouble. Returning home after a particularly urgent and difficult house-call, a volunteer discovered that in his haste he had not brought his house keys with him. He too was picked up by the police, trying to climb into his own house via the drainpipe. Some explanation was required, not an easy matter for a member of an organisation which at that time had very strong rules against revealing that one was a Samaritan. This was so strongly felt that in one branch the director was referred to in a rather sinister fashion as *Mr X*.

Shirley from Leeds tells of the occasion when she and a younger colleague (at least on this occasion a man and a woman went, by no means always the case), were sent to a high-rise block to help a psychiatric patient who had discharged himself from hospital but found he couldn't cope. There was no phone and there was a high wind so that she felt the block swaying, but she had to stay with the caller while her colleague went off to see if he could get the man re-admitted. The choice between the hazards of Leeds' streets on a dark night and a seriously disturbed male caller had to be weighed up but she stayed. While they were waiting the caller said to her, *"would you like to look in my suitcase?"*.

It proved to contain a whole collection of winceyette knickers of the old-fashioned *passion-killer* type. Another branch had a regular visitor, now long dead, who used to bring in a suitcase full of rubber bathing caps and aprons. He had no-one else to share with.

On a night shift in a large city branch there was a ring at the back door late at night. The door opened to reveal a mother with four small children. Although

it was unusual even then, the circumstances suggested that she should come in, which she did, leaving the pram outside, despite a warning of *"at your own risk"* from the volunteers. Well into the befriending interview, another ring came at the back door. This was quite unprecedented and the volunteers on duty enquired, somewhat nervously who was there. *"It's the police!"* came a deep voice in reply. *"How do we know who you are?"* *"I'll put my truncheon through the letterbox!"* A policeman with a sense of humour obviously! Worse was to follow for he had come to say that a baby had been abandoned on the doorstep. After an initial reaction of horror it was realised that the caller had not only left the pram but also the baby, (a fifth child), outside the door, in a very dubious area. On this occasion all was resolved and the policeman helped the caller to get home under his protection.

Some of the caller stories which can be told (confidentiality means a strict ban on any personal revealing details) are very touching. A very long-standing caller who visited a centre regularly used to come with his flea-ridden dog. (Maybe this was not as strange as the visitor to the Boston centre in the States who used to bring his pet pig.) The sad part of it came on the day when he arrived with the dog dead, carried in a black wheely bin. He just had nowhere else to turn to help him with this tragedy.

Early callers to the Luton branch are recorded bringing dogs, but one even brought a Siamese cat. In Bournemouth one such pet even helped with the work. A volunteer was in the habit of bringing her dog, a standard poodle, to the centre when she was on shift. One day a *charming old gentleman* in a state of great distress came to the door. As space was limited, the volunteer had to take him into the main office. (Something unthinkable today!) A little later she was

called away for a short time but when she returned she found Caspar, the dog, sitting on the settee beside the caller who had both arms around its neck and was quietly weeping into its fur. A little later he got up and said he felt much better. Who was the Samaritan that day?

On one occasion in Leeds the volunteer on duty was startled when she opened the door and found on the step a clown in full rig and make-up, with a large red nose. He had cracked up while working in Blackpool and fled. In another centre, a caller left alone for a moment while the volunteer made him a cup of tea, wandered off and found an unattended phone from which he made a hoax call to the fire-brigade. Imagine the red faces!

In those days it was common for callers to be *befriended* in their own home.

When there was an emergency call two people would normally be sent, but under the system of one-to-one befriending volunteers could become quite involved in their callers' lives. It was only in the 70s and after, that this practice began to be seen as risky and such befriendings were never done solo. In any case a befriending was not expected to last forever, only for the duration of the client's crisis, a principle which still endures. One volunteer, Joan, was asked by her *befriendee* whether she could feed her pet while she went away for a few days. *"Certainly, no trouble"*, responded the volunteer only to discover to her horror that the pet in question was a particularly vicious goose. Another example of pro-active pet-minding was the Samaritan care offered to a caller's disabled budgie which used to spend its holidays with them while its owner went to see her father in South Africa. It is not on record whether they managed to teach it to say *"Samaritans. Can we help you?"*

Even in the safety of their own centres there were adventures to be had. Tales abound of callers arriving brandishing axes and several centres have been attacked over the years with bricks and other missiles. Others in vulnerable areas such as Newry and Omagh have been badly damaged by bombs, though this was not the result of caller activity. One man arrived at a centre highly distressed and covered in cuts and cigarette burns. He explained that he had broken out of a secure psychiatric unit. Indeed he had - straight through a plate glass window.

In our modern technological age, some branches have felt the need to instal CCTV in order to monitor the front of the premises. In one such a volunteer quietly befriending a suicidal caller suddenly became aware of a close relative of *"the Incredible Hulk"* thrusting a muscular arm through the front of the building which was made of boarding. A second arm followed, but fortunately, the owner apparently had had enough at this point and left.

Many centres in the early days had to be closed down for certain times of the day. At that time there was no technology for transferring calls unless by a landline from one centre to another. The cost of this was prohibitive and the norm was to transfer the phone to a volunteer's home. In theory this might have been acceptable, though the recipient would be very much on their own with the calls, but there was a great drawback. The operator would intercept the call to the branch and tell the caller to dial again on another number - that of the volunteer's home. So much for anonymity, as one branch director found to her cost when a caller, who had chronic problems, recognised her voice and remembered her number - for the next 20 years.

Former chairman Albert Jewell remembers his early days. *"In those days (1965) I was recruited directly by the local rector, (who was also the branch director) in a town which shall be nameless. There was minimal preparation and on-going training. Volunteers were only required in the evenings, overnight and at weekends - because the rector's secretary took the calls between 9 am and 5.30 pm on weekdays. Calls overnight were switched to your own home. So that if the phone rang after 10 pm, you never knew whether it would be a caller or your mother-in-law. As you also doubled as flying squad you might have to leave your other half to take any subsequent calls and deliver the shocking news that the Samaritan was out at present!"*

Working conditions

In the early days, many branches worked in incredibly uncomfortable and difficult circumstances. Few had any financial resources when they started up and had to rely on the generosity of local people. In many cases this meant taking on premises loaned or rented at a very low price by a local church or the local council. The Torbay and South Devon branch was first set up in a small room which was an annexe to the vicarage of All Saints, Babbacombe, whose vicar, Father Tony Andrews was the first director. In Bolton, it was a church vestry behind the organ which provided the first premises.

In Bath the first initiative to call an open meeting came from the rector of Bath Abbey, so the first centre was Abbey Church House where it stayed until, in 1967, a property was rented in Henry Street. This consisted of two tiny rooms on the fourth floor, described as *bijou* by one volunteer. The first room had a phone, a notice-board, one desk and a chair. Its single window and low ceiling must have been quite claustrophobic. The second room was kept for befriending visitors. At that time it cost £300 per annum to run the branch. Later the branch found a new home in King Street. This was a great improvement if one forgets the fact that the roof leaked. In order to protect confidentiality it was decided to do an *in-house*

The duty room in St Paul's New Cross, Manchester about 1966. Chad and Basil Higginson with volunteer Freda

job on re-roofing the building using the expertise of a builder who was a former caller. This was very dangerous with a 50 foot drop and sharp railings around the area steps. Just as an aside it is worth noting that one branch, which allowed AA to use its meeting room was taken to court by one of the members of that organisation who had carelessly fallen down their area steps. Needless to say, they were not inclined to lend their room to anyone else.

Manchester's first permanent centre after a spell of doing overnight shifts above a dry cleaner's shop, where volunteers were often stopped and interviewed by police patrols who thought they were up to no good, was a transept and one aisle of St Paul's Church in New Cross. It was infested by mice and rats so Samantha, the branch cat, was recruited. At night she could be heard engaged in her nocturnal pursuit and the scufflings and squeaks could be quite alarming. On one occasion as a volunteer was talking to a seriously depressed caller on the phone a mouse appeared with Samantha in hot pursuit. The two then proceeded to run round and round the telephone table under the feet of the volunteer.

The lavatory, referred to by early volunteers as *the Château d'If*, was in the crypt. The sinister shadows cast by the broken and discarded pews stacked up there were thought to harbour all kinds of nasties. To venture down, especially in the dark, could be an alarming experience. The problem came to an end when the loo fell through the floor. (No-one was on it at the time!) After this disaster the only option was the public facility round the corner. This was fine except on Sunday afternoon when, for some unfathomable reason, the council shut the ladies' lavatories at 4 pm. This, needless to say did not apply to the gents! One advantage of working in these conditions was the wonderful singing, which the Sunday morning shift could listen to as the church was used by a local Russian Orthodox congregation.

Speaking of lavatories, at Luton in the early days the loo was at the very top of an overgrown garden set amongst derelict houses. Volunteers were sure they would encounter rats. At first the only light available at night was a candle until some thoughtful person provided a torch. It was not unusual to make the call armed with torch and brolly, in case of wildlife and in the winter, the cistern froze. These premises were kindly loaned to the branch and consisted of a single room in a house between two others used by other groups, one of which, if memory serves correctly was the *Moral Welfare Society*, not a great advert for the non-judgmental nature of Samaritan work. Volunteers going on duty here were so depressed by the nature of the pictures on display such as *the Stag at Bay* and *the Crown of Thorns* that they used to cover them up with an old

MAYORESS SEES HOW SAMARITANS WORK

SINCE January 1, the Luton Samaritans, the organisation that helps people in distress or despair, have been offering a 24-hour emergency service.

On Friday, the Mayoress of Luton, Mrs. Lynda Macdonald, visited the Samaritans premises at 67 Adelaide Street, to see how the organisation is run.

Also present was Mr. Basil Higginson, general secretary of the National Samaritan Organisation.

While the Mayoress was at the premises she received a message of congratulations on the 24-hour service on behalf of the Luton branch from Mr. David Arthur, vice-chairman of the Samaritans Incorporated, who was phoning from Stirling in Scotland.

Mr. Higginson said there are now 101 branches in Britain and 10 overseas.

"It is noticeable that the suicide rate is lower in those towns with a Samaritan branch," he said.

He also congratulated the Luton Samaritans which he said was one of the most active branches in the country.

Our picture (AW8011R) shows the Mayoress on the phone to Mr. Arthur, while the Rev. David Clendon, director of Luton Samaritans, looks on.

curtain whenever they were on shifts. At Stockport the first centre was a small terraced house, kindly leased at peppercorn rent by the corporation. When it was taken on it was completely derelict and due for demolition. In fact when the electricity board was asked to reconnect the power they replied that the property had been pulled down. They had removed the ring-main. The building department of the nearby college did the repairs and decorations but their ministrations did not prevent a rich crop of black mould gradually crawling up the walls. By a curious coincidence at the opening ceremony the Lady Mayoress exclaimed, *"I'm so glad to see this house put to such good use. I was brought up here!"*

Another branch, Cheltenham, was also, like many others, opened by the Mayor who was to make the very first call to the newborn branch. He dialled a number only to be told by the operator that it was the wrong one and offered the one that he needed.

Similarly, Horsham and Crawley branch were dependent upon the generosity of their local authority for their first premises. As beggars couldn't be choosers, the delightful smells emanating from their neighbours had to be ignored if not endured. On one side was a grain store which encouraged a large rat population, and the olfactory ambiance was enhanced by the rag and bone yard on the other side.

Even more recently-founded branches such as Stornoway in the Western Isles report that their early premises were damp and creaky. A visitor from Inverness reported sounds of heavy breathing from next door, a property which had been empty for many

years. This seems to echo the branch in the Southern region which is convinced that the premises are haunted since the bedroom in which volunteers sleep on peaceful overnight duties, (this is a fairly quiet branch) seems to contain a presence which can be alarming.

HRH the Duchess of Kent opens the present Manchester centre in 1993

Beds are not always safe either. In Southend, a volunteer on night duty was taking a call while lying on the piece of furniture provided for the purpose, found herself completely enfolded in the grip of the zed-bed which had collapsed in on itself. Fortunately both caller and volunteer ended the call in helpless laughter.

In some areas it was reaching the centre which was (and may still be) hazardous. Stepping over the pools of blood and vomit on the pavement after a Saturday overnight shift might well be a normal part of the work. In at least one case the branch, in its early days, was situated in the red light district, so any female volunteer tempted to wait outside for her lift home would be told, *"don't stand around outside like that or you'll have your eyes scratched out"*. Similarly the centre situated across the road from a sex shop had a good deal of free entertainment when there was a police raid. A visiting volunteer from a neighbouring branch was fascinated by the activity opposite. *"Oh look, there's someone coming out!"* A brief pause ensued, then, *"oh dear, they're from our branch!"* When the same centre was visited by HRH the Duchess of Kent, then the royal patron of The Samaritans, some of the excellently clear press photographs were somewhat marred by the words *Private Shop* writ large above the royal head.

When Manchester worked from the church building the caretaker would come on Sunday morning waving a filthy milk bottle and shouting, *"one of your men has used the church porch as a toilet again"*. She did not mean a volunteer of course. Most branches received visits from many *Gentlemen of the road* in the old days. These often moved from branch to branch and would report on their reception, frequently critically, at the last port of call. The were nick-named the *Tea Set* or *the Tea Brigade* in many branches. Some would demand, in thick and perhaps slurred accents, *tea and biscuits* but there were few as unassuming as *Tony the*

Tramp who lived in a doorway across the road from a centre. He would arrive with a dried up much-used teabag and ask for some water to add to it. Needless to say, most volunteers produced a new teabag as well. One visitor at Bristol used to say that he came to the branch because it was the only place he was treated as a human being. Another regular visitor to one centre used to bring an invisible friend with him to whom he used to talk about a wide range of current issues, usually in an apparently aggressive manner. He, or rather they, used to drop in often for a cup of tea and to set the world to rights. He was a familiar sight (and sound) in the neighbouring streets and it did seem sad somehow when the medical authorities caught up with him. His friend disappeared under treatment but left him a pathetic shadow of his former self. He never came to the centre after that.

Kerry branch before... (A total of £40,000 was raised to buy and renovate the house)

Another caller of no fixed abode used to pop into his local centre late in the evening and demand accommodation. When this was not forthcoming, he would throw a handful of pills triumphantly into his mouth exclaiming, *"now you'll have to get me into hospital!"*.

Then there was the scruffily dignified caller who made a habit of touring the country, asking each branch for tea and biscuits while he did his correspondence. He was an inveterate letter writer to all the great and the good of the country. Who knows what he wrote about, but he would become haughtily aggressive if crossed. He also knew every parson in each location he visited and could

...and after

frequently be seen sitting on some unfortunate reverend's doorstep. On one occasion an elderly volunteer to her horror, found him, as she thought, on her step until she realised he was visiting the minister who lived next door. She beat a hasty retreat until he had left.

At least these familiar visitors were not difficult, and some had touching stories. Others though were quite demanding, not of befriending, but more practical things like money and there have, on occasions been less welcome guests. Many centres have had their windows broken or their front entrances damaged and more than one caller has attempted to set premises on fire. One visitor had severe psychotic problems and volunteers were warned not to smile at him if he arrived on the doorstep as this would enrage him. It was not so easy to implement this as a welcoming smile would be the volunteers' habitual approach. At Luton a volunteer recalls that on only her third duty someone arrived on the doorstep having ingested a bottle of tablets. The facilities of the branch at that time being strictly limited, the volunteer took him into the only available room where he was promptly very sick over the daily log book, which the volunteer notes *"was good for him but we found made a mess of our book!"*.

In one Lancashire branch a caller frequently rang to say that he had left a bomb in the centre, always shortly after he had actually visited. Young Julie, aged only 17, had a habit of gouging out deep lines on the sides of expensive cars parked around the streets, (when she was not carving her initials in her own flesh). Gradually she came to trust her local branch and actually asked them for a list of their volunteers' registration numbers so that she could avoid damaging any Samaritan cars. Needless to say, this was not forthcoming!

There has always been a debate in branches about how much security is required and, despite times when callers have leapt over counters or broken down locked doors, there have been relatively few incidents of a serious nature. Nowadays, though, there is a heightened awareness of health and safety issues and it is more common for branches to think about security measures such as CCTV and personal alarms. It seems a pity, but one must move with the times. Below is an experience at Hull branch by described by Audrey 1, in *The Samaritan*.

How we got our own back

So much planning, so much hard work over so many years had finally resulted in the best ever Samaritan centre. An old house eviscerated, reshaped and embalmed, and entirely suited to its purpose was ready to be furnished and made worthy of the suicidal and despairing who would come to talk, to cry or to absorb the unhurried silence within its walls. To be worthy too of the 150 or more men and women who would listen and befriend at all hours of the day or night. Because already £1,200 had been spent, (the result of nine years of charity shops, sponsored walks, coffee mornings, concerts, appeals to churches, societies, individuals), one Samaritan set out to test the results of begging. So every large store, dozens of small shops, factories, and warehouses received letters. Many firms and individuals responded. One firm not only sent carpets but also their fitters to lay them. Others gave gas fires, cooker, lamps, curtain material, electric kettles, typewriters, a hoover, sheets, blankets and pillows, and even toilet rolls and tissues.

When 4 September, the day of the official opening, arrived, it was unbelievably lovely, with magnificent floral displays and plants in every room. It was not surprising that the local radio referred to 'the luxurious premises of The Samaritans'.

"the luxurious premises of The Samaritans"

Were the fates murmuring something about pride going before a fall?

A few days later, the one scheduled for the "at home" for doctors and others to come and see before the actual transfer of work, the secretary was shocked to find that we had been burgled. All our best rugs and expensive equipment, and even the toilet rolls had gone. Everyone was shocked, the press, the police and our supporters were very angry. Offers of help poured in…but one real friend came secretly, asked what had gone and said "leave it to me".

All through the night he worked hard. He sent out his friends to the haunts that only they knew. Before daylight, they had found the man, dealt with him in their own way and made him reveal where everything was. So, in the early hours of the morning the possessions began to come back, rugs, cups, carpets, telephones, sheets and the hoover. Yes, even the tissues and toilet rolls: all formed one large heap in the middle of the toilet floor. Our tired friend and his associates went to their well-earned rest and we rejoiced.

Keeping up the standard

In the early days there was a variable amount and quality of training offered to potential volunteers. In some branches they were recruited by their local vicar and were offered little or no actual training in the work while in others, such as Portsmouth, where John Eldrid followed the style of the original London centre, there was an actual programme of training offered as the following document shows:

The Samaritans (Portsmouth Branch)

The purpose of this group of people is to bring help to those in despair and contemplating suicide. A telephone in the centre in the Parish Hall of "All Saints" is manned day and night, and the number will be widely publicised in the city.

Those who join the volunteer force for this work will receive training (not at first exceeding 6 to 8 sessions) and will be expected to do turns of duty aggregating 24 hours a month. In general they will extend to persons who contact us friendship and care. These clients will normally be referred to the priest or other person on duty.

There will be several priests or ministers acting as spiritual advisers - one always on call. In addition there will be a psychiatrist consultant and other specialists.

The strictest confidence will, of course, be kept regarding anything which may be known of the client's affairs.

We shall be glad to know of those who wish to volunteer for this important work. The main qualification is love and care for people, and a desire to help and be sympathetic to them in their distress.

It is noteworthy that at this stage, about 1963, there was still an assumption that *the professionals* would expect to be involved in the support of those who called. The implication that the *ordinary* volunteers would only act as an initial contact and provide a referral mechanism seems to be clear. By the late 60s this idea was dying out and, as preparation for the work became standard,

Preparation used to consist of a series of lectures

volunteers would be fully involved in befriending all callers.

In many branches the first stages were different. In at least one branch the only training offered was the provision of a folder of material for reference. Dorothy of Bristol remembers hearing about *General browsing*, and thinking it was a person. In fact it contained all the volunteer should know about how to do the work.

In those early days much of the information related to which consultant professional should be called in the face of any difficulty. It was quite common to be invited into the centre, as Dorothy remembers, for a chat with someone of standing in the branch and then to be told, *"please attend for your first duty on Thursday week at 10.30"*. Many other volunteers recall something similar. *"Oh and by the way, if you want, there are some lectures on a Wednesday evening you can come to as well."* This lead to inconsistencies between branches. At least one of the new regional training officers appointed in the mid-80s had herself received no training when she joined her branch in 1966, though she had of course made up for the lack in the intervening years.

The lectures provided reflected a concern with the idea that volunteers needed a certain depth of knowledge about the kinds of problem, which might be encountered. Lectures on topics such as *endogenous depression, psychotic illness* and even perhaps a lecture by the local pharmacist about drugs used for clinical purposes which a caller might have taken in order to commit suicide, used to be common. In many branches where there was a strong clergy presence it was the theory of *Clinical Theology*, which had a great following in the early 60s, which figured in the training of volunteers. This explained depressive illness and various forms of addiction in terms of spiritual difficulties.

The following programme was offered to volunteers who were accepted to work in the new Portsmouth branch in 1963:

TRAINING OF SAMARITANS - Stage 1.

Wednesday

24th Oct.

1. The telephone Drill - talking, listening, and referring.
How we envisage the scheme working and explanation of rota.

31st Oct.

2. The Background - Psychological
Simple talk by a Psychologist

7th Nov.

3. The Background - Medical
A panel of Doctors - how it ties up with the Doctor's work.

14th Nov.

4. The Background - Social, Welfare State etc.

21st Nov.

5. The Background - Spiritual
Spiritual resources available. What the priest can do.

28th Nov.

6. How to help by befriending.

5th Dec.

7. A further session on befriending.

12th Dec.

8. Any questions? Revision

Training periods will last one and a quarter hours. Talk or demonstration followed by discussion.

This programme clearly shows the involvement of professionals and the emphasis on knowledge.

When Blackburn branch began in 1969 the outline programme for preparation classes was designed to take five weeks. The first and second of these were given by the director, who was a consultant psychiatrist, and covered *general principles and befriending* and *psychological problems*. Week three was presented by Rev. Cragg *(sic)* and dealt with sexual problems. Week four came from a marriage

73

guidance counsellor and was about marital problems. (Odd that these two weeks were not seen to overlap.) The final week came from Mr Eastwood of the Information Bureau and looked at the *Relationships of the statutory and voluntary bodies*. There seems to have been no room for interaction or feedback from the new volunteers.

An important change came into being during the 1970s. The word used to describe the induction process was changed from *training* to *preparation* on the grounds that the four qualities of caring, willingness to share the callers' suffering, and the emotional strength to bear it, the ability to respond with sensitivity and the ability to accept all that might be encountered were the requirements for Samaritan work. The first

Ongoing training must attract its students

two are inborn, the last two can be developed if a volunteer is properly prepared for what the work entails. Listening skills, the ability to hear both what is being said and the space between the words, provide the core of the service.

It was Roy Vining, the Lowestoft GP who also played an important role in the development of Samaritan thinking on suicide, who produced the first materials for preparation classes as well as for on-going training. He collected from branches which had already pioneered new techniques, a huge range of resources designed to break away from the lecture format and to provide activities in which the volunteers would participate. This was at a time when even in education (which should have known better!) in-service training often consisted of dreary talks accompanied by illegible overhead projector transparencies.

Roy's *Training Samaritans* published in 1981 provided the inspiration for a radical change, and his *Compendium of case study material* contained a wealth of scenarios for use in both types of preparation and training. A vote by the Council of Management in 1981 making the attendance at on-going training compulsory, later made even more specific by the requirement for each volunteer to do five hours per year, made this set of resources invaluable to those who had to deliver the programmes. Activities such as *the goldfish bowl, machine gun, the flying circus* and *poster pairs* made classes much more exciting, though the much-dreaded *role play* has never been a favourite, despite its being a very valuable way of gaining experience. In some branches the process was rigorous. Mike Charman wrote, in 1970, of a session he attended at the Central London branch on *sensitivity testing* that it was *"The most nerve-wracking experience that I have had for many a long day. I was totally astonished at the nerve of, in particular, the three young ladies...There is little doubt that if the London Volunteers can get through this, they will have little difficulty in coping with the most extremely depressed and suicidal clients."*

In 1985 the first national co-ordinator for training was appointed. This was Norman Whiting of Grantham, whose experience in education made him ideal for the job. His work, and that of his successor, Joan Guénault of Lancaster led to a standardisation of all aspects of training which in turn helped to bring about consistency in the service offered by different branches. Large red ring binders full of training materials began to appear in branches at this time, the first being *the suicide question*, the most fundamental issue to be covered. Subsequent packs have included, *follow-up, third party calls* and many others.

Norman's gentle wit encouraged many to introduce humour into classes as well as into national training schools and conferences. Writing in *'Samaritan News'* Issue Number 1 in April 1986 he mused on what further training of volunteers should be called. Should it be **ONGOT** - short for On-going training, or perhaps **INSERT** - In-service training - though he felt this sounded rather painful. Perhaps **CONTROV**, Continued training of volunteers had a whiff of authoritarianism about it. Much more friendly is the social aspect of training emphasised by those branches offering **VODKAS** - Volunteer

Norman Whiting

development in knowledge. But this is likely to be misunderstood...as is the simple formula *Further preparation of volunteers* since the acronym FUPOV may be mistaken for the volunteers' response when asked to participate.

At least one region published a resource file entitled *Have you had your MOT-*

Marvellous Ongoing Training. The quality of Samaritan preparation and training became the object of much admiration amongst other professional bodies and in 1991 Joan Guénault was presented with an award in recognition of its outstanding quality. There are many people, current and former Samaritan volunteers who would say that hardly a day passes without their using their Samaritan training.

Over the years many thousands of volunteers have benefited from the various schools and conferences available both nationally and locally. No account of Samaritan history can be complete without a reference to the *Swanwicks* which many a director or other office-bearer attended. In the

Joan Guénault

60s, 70s and early 80s, these were a real experience, not to say a challenge. Having first passed the scrutiny of the guardian of the registration desk, Jean

Jean Archer

Archer, the first step was to find one's room in the labyrinthine conference centre plan. If one was unlucky, this might be at the far side of the estate in the wooden Garden House. This was renowned for its chilliness in winter and, as there was a January school each year, thermal undies were a *must*. There were adventures to be had sometimes. One volunteer had to climb in through a window to help out a colleague who had lost her key. Another, blind, volunteer was nearly frightened to death when, as the fire alarm started to ring, several strange people rushed into and through her bedroom. She had been placed in the room with the fire-escape. At meal times the trick was to make sure that one was not at the serving end of the table. Dividing the communal dishes into 20 portions required the skills of a geometrician. Meals were further enlivened by the military-style announcements made over a loudspeaker by Wally Milne who was, for many years, in charge of the conference centre. These might go as follows: *"The first SIX tables at tonight's meal will be vegetarian. If you do not like curry sit at the seventh to the tenth table. If you wish to have your chicken curried, sit at tables eleven to twenty…"* and so on. The evening newspaper announcement was also typical: *"If you would like a newspaper tomorrow, please order now. If you*

Swanwick

would like The Times, *raise your hand. If you would like the* Telegraph, *raise your hand now. If you would like the* Guardian, *raise your hand now. If you would like the* Mail...*but I don't think we'll go any further down..."* Much of the food in those days was grown on the premises, but many will perhaps prefer not to remember some of the cuisine at that time. Having said this, the main hall had great character in those days, being furnished with Lloyd Loom chairs, at least in the middle block, where the great and the good, such as Doris Odlum, George Day and the Executive Committee members always sat. Many happy hours could be spent queuing at the bar or socialising in the Vinery, which really had its own vine. Now the centre has been modernised, it seems to have lost some of its charms, but it is at least warm and comfortable.

The annual conference, nowadays always held at York, is a great experience as well as a learning opportunity. To see for the first time, the Great Hall filled with over a thousand Samaritans, of all ages, backgrounds and origins, united in one purpose and to realise one's place in a worldwide movement is unforgettable.

Behind the mask

Callers and members of the general public sometimes preface their remarks with a question. *"Is that the good Samaritans?"* How does one respond? *"No, we're not good"*, perhaps? The confusion of the organisation's name with the biblical story is natural, but quite mistaken. For one thing, Samaritans do not *do* as the biblical character did. They may offer help where others may *"pass by on the other side"*, but that help comes in the form of constructive and supportive listening. The aim is not to live other people's lives for them, or to wave a magic wand and solve their problems, but rather to help them to face up to their situation in such a way that their quality of life may begin to improve. In any case, the members are not saints, nor are their own lives perfect. Today's volunteer might be tomorrow's caller, or vice versa. It is only a small step from one side of the telephone to the other and indeed, it is the very fact of shared humanity, with all its weaknesses as well as its strengths which makes the process work.

So what is it like to be a Samaritan? Why do people volunteer in the first place, and why do they stay?

Picture this, it is 3 am on a cold winter's night in the middle of a large city; there is a light in an upstairs window. There, in a low-lit office two people are responding softly into telephone receivers. Not much of what is being said can be heard, as it is the callers who are doing most of the talking. This is the night shift in the local Samaritan branch. These volunteers have been here since 11 pm and for the last four hours they have been listening to people with all kinds of problems. Maybe someone is sitting at home with a bottle of pills and a pint of whisky to help them down. Can that phone call literally make the difference between life and death? Some of the calls are less dramatic but still draining.

Many of those who call are very depressed and take long pauses between each word. It may be that the caller is in a high state of distress and unable to explain clearly what he or she is feeling. There are still four and a half hours to go and as the sounds of merriment from the revellers turning out of the clubs drift upwards from the street the

A good night's sleep in your own bed is welcome after an overnight duty

Volunteers come from all kinds of background

volunteers continue to listen to the sad, lonely and suicidal. They will probably be busy until they knock off at 7.30 am, maybe not even able to have a break to go and make a cup of coffee, and sometimes it can even be a problem to find time for a loo visit. No sleep for them tonight!

So why put oneself through this kind of gruelling session for no pay? If one did a survey of all the motives which prompt individuals to volunteer as Samaritans, the responses would be as varied as the people you asked. Volunteers come from all kinds of background. They may have exciting jobs or they may be students, or unemployed, or retired. They may live in big houses or small ones or in scruffy bed sits. They may be 18 or 80 or any age in between.

Many Samaritan volunteers join because somewhere in their lives they have seen trouble. This may be their own experience of depression or bereavement or illness or it may be that of a close relative or friend. They feel that they may have a special insight into how others may feel. (It is important, though, not to say, *"I know exactly how you feel"*. No-one can ever know exactly, but it is possible to have some empathy or imaginative insight.)

Others have come to a crossroads in their lives where they find they have some time to spare. Perhaps the family has grown up and left home, or a course has finished or retirement has been reached. Some will say that they have been considering joining for a long time and that now the moment has come.

As we have seen, despite the name it is not a religious organisation but there are volunteers from many faiths including Christian, Jewish, Muslim, Buddhist and Hindu. Their motives may be due to deep religious conviction. There are others who would say they have no religious belief, but they do feel some sense of responsibility to fellow human beings.

For very many volunteers the

Samaritans are known to have the occasional get-together

79

reason is simple. They feel that life has been good to them and that it is time to put something back. Many are reluctant to say that they enjoy the work since this seems to imply that they revel in other people's suffering. This is certainly not the case, and there is nothing wrong in saying that the work is *rewarding*. There may be shifts when the volunteer comes out feeling that they haven't been able to help anyone, but on other occasions there will have been one call (or many) from which the listener comes out saying *"I'm so glad I was there for that person"*. These volunteers do not ask for thanks, but it is a great feeling when someone says that they have really been helped to face tomorrow because of their contact with The Samaritans.

There is another side, a lighter aspect, to being a Samaritan. To begin with, the whole ethos of the organisation creates strong bonds between its members. Each member should feel supported, whether on shift, or in their own lives, and, for many, their strongest friendships have been forged through their shared interest in the work. Each branch has its own approach to social events which may be seen as a way of bonding the team more closely, and it is common for a party to be held to celebrate an anniversary or to thank a member, such as a retiring director, for particular service to the branch. On these occasions the impressive level of creativity which goes into decorating commemorative cakes is amazing.

Dennis, the mobile befriending centre in action in Covent Garden, London

Like most other charities, branches need money and fund-raising events are part of the work. These too can be highly imaginative, or purely physical but they perform a dual service, that of bringing in funds and that of raising public awareness of the service. Public appearances in such contexts as carnivals or civic parades were rare before the 80s and it was remarked by many of the volunteers who took part in such activities how warmly the public responded to them. Their very visibility, after decades of complete facelessness paid dividends.

Not all of those who volunteer as Samaritans enjoy taking part in this kind of activity. Some feel that this is not why they joined. For this reason some branches began to recruit Friends, formally constituted groups whose sole *raison d'être* was to raise money. These non-listening volunteers have given invaluable service over the years and are sometimes unsung heroes. In some places there are dedicated teams who run charity shops raising money for The Samaritans and their existence helps to bring the name into the High Street.

Sally, chairman of Friends, shuts up shop in Bridlington

Unsung heroes

Emily: a typical volunteer

In 1989 one of the oldest Samaritan volunteers hung up the phone for the last time at the age of 87. She was typical of so many of the early volunteers in that she came to Samaritan work through her contact with the church. Her new vicar was in need of a temporary home while the vicarage was being rebuilt. And she, a single lady who had lived alone since the death of her parents, had space to offer. At that time he was involved in helping to set up a branch of The Samaritans with two other clergy. One day he said to her, *"We need a Samaritan to handle calls at lunchtime. Could you do it?"*. Though a little taken aback, Emily accepted the challenge and continued in the work until she had put in an incredible 12,000 hours of helping. She was a founder member of her branch and a totally modest and unassuming person. As she got older she used to say to her director, *"You will tell me when I'm past it, won't you?"* to which the response was, *"As long as you are asking, you are not!"* In fact she knew herself when the time had finally come to retire as her hearing began to fail and the journey on the bus became too much. Her gentle voice and warmth must have helped hundreds of callers, and she recalled that the types of call had changed over the years. Her first call was about a practical matter; how a widow could claim her pension. Latterly the calls became much more challenging, covering the full range of human emotion. She was also aware that increasingly the group most at risk was younger than it had been earlier in her Samaritan career. Like many of her colleagues, she had, sadly, lost a caller by suicide despite her best efforts. The caller had taken an overdose, but left it too late to pass on her personal details and to agree to let Emily call an ambulance. As every Samaritan who has this experience knows, all one can

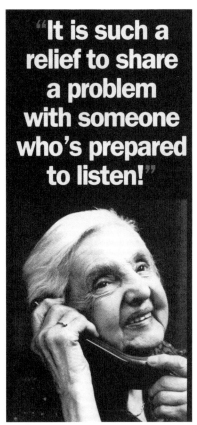

"It is such a relief to share a problem with someone who's prepared to listen!"

Emily

say is, as Emily herself said, *"I tried my best - it just wasn't good enough, but you have to console yourself that no matter how hard you try, you can't save every caller threatening suicide"*. Samaritan Principle Three allows the caller the choice between life and death, however hard it is to accept it when the caller takes the latter path. Despite her modesty, Emily's story was taken up by *Bella* magazine who described her life and career at the time of her retirement. The accompanying picture was adopted by the Samaritan national publicity team and figured in a number of items of national publicity, including that for older callers. She was quite amazed by this high profile as she was the very last person to wish for it. It has been a great privilege for colleagues to have known people of such dedication as Emily, and the very many other volunteers like her who give unstintingly of their time and care for many years without expecting any kind of reward except the satisfaction of feeling that other people have been helped through their efforts.

To see ourselves as others...

Anonymity may have been the watchword for ordinary volunteers, but there is little point in offering a service if no-one is aware of its existence. The Founder always said that *"publicity is the life-blood of the movement"* and certainly without it, the work would have fizzled and died.

In fact, successive studies researching into the level of public awareness have shown that the name *Samaritans* has a very high recognition factor amongst those surveyed, ranging between 80 and 98 per cent. The work of David Merritt Jackson and Rex Cannon introduced the idea of a Samaritan identity which would be recognised by the public.

Over the years there have been many references to The Samaritans and their work in all areas of the media. Frequently cartoons appear poking fun, usually gently, at the work. Sometimes volunteers themselves produce them (a sense of humour is an absolute essential).

Private Eye and *Punch* have frequently published cartoons, reflecting the fact that those who read the magazines would understand the references. Similarly, in sitcoms and series, there are jokes about The Samaritans. In at least two episodes of *Fawlty Towers* Basil uses the name to get himself out of a sticky situation, as when his formidable wife, Sybil, catches him about to talk to his bookie. *"Just ringing The Samaritans, dear"*, he says. On another occasion, he is discovered in an unusually sunny mood, humming to himself. Sybil is immediately suspicious. *"It's just my way of getting through the day. The Samaritans were busy."*

1983 Christmas card from Private Eye, *reproduced by kind permission in* The Samaritan *magazine*

Recognition is one thing, but understanding of exactly what is offered is another. There is a generally benevolent attitude towards the organisation. *"They do a good job"* is a common reaction, but when people are asked if they would use the service, the response may be different. They may say, *"I'm not that bad"*, *"I'm not suicidal"* or even, *"I never thought of it"*. The truth may go deeper. No-one wants to feel that they are out of control of their lives, still less to admit it. Any volunteer would recognise the guilt which can accompany a first call. *"I've always been able to cope. Everyone depends on me. I shouldn't have to ask for help."*

In order to overcome this kind of barrier, there have been many approaches to publicising the work. Sometimes this has been through radio or television programmes initiated by the media themselves. Sometimes, also, the publicity has not always been quite as positive as it could have been. Many years ago in *The Archers* for example, the local vicar was a volunteer. All well and good until some controversy arose over a matter about which he had become aware through a call while he was on duty. His subsequent actions gave the impression that Samaritan confidentiality was not absolute. Naturally, representations were made for this to be corrected in a later programme.

The service has figured in several TV soaps too. *Coronation Street* has had more than one suicidal character and in *Eastenders* one of the characters was a volunteer, but the biggest television exposure came in 1971 with the transmission of a series called *The Befrienders* about a fictional Samaritans branch. This was the work largely of Harry Junkin and had a cast of well-known actors. It was much enjoyed by many and certainly led to an expansion both in recruitment and in caller rates, but a BBC survey of audience reaction was not altogether favourable, mainly on the grounds that it was rather slow. The drama was inclined to be low-key, and there is no doubt that some volunteers were a little sceptical since they considered parts of it over-romanticised. Chad certainly believed that it was volunteer response which killed the possibility of a further series, but the evidence does not seem to reflect this. The tapes, in accordance with the practice of the day, were wiped so there is no chance to reassess the merits of the series. Without doubt, however, it brought Samaritans

"I'm going through a rather sticky period, so I thought it wise to put them on a retainer."

Reprinted by kind permission of Punch in The Samaritan *magazine*

85

(Provenance unknown)

out of the shadows and produced genuine public sympathy.

In later years there have been documentary programmes on radio, for example when the Pendle branch preparation class was featured, and on television when a crew spent an overnight shift with the Birmingham branch. Volunteers tend to be oversensitive about the images which are recorded. This may reflect the residue of the strong taboo on breaching anonymity, but for much of the public it provides a welcome, and impressive, insight into Samaritan work. After the Birmingham programme a work colleague said to a volunteer, *"I never realised till I saw that programme that you Samaritans REALLY care"*. If public exposure leads to this kind of response, it must be accepted as a good thing.

Cartoon reprinted from The Samaritan *where it was reproduced by kind permission of* Private Eye

Does it work?

Any organisation in receipt of public money can, in the 21st century, expect to be accountable. This is generally assumed to be achievable by presenting facts and figures regarding the *consumers* and their degree of satisfaction with the service provided. This apparently straightforward task is one which presents The Samaritans with great difficulties. Confidentiality means that no detailed report can be made on those who make contact and in any case outcomes are seldom known. Thanks are not expected and are rarely offered. Thus self-evaluation is difficult and evidence can only be anecdotal based on caller rates.

Having said this, there have been attempts over the years to prove the value of the work. In the 60s, Dr Richard Fox and other psychiatrists presented many papers to various professional bodies which debated reasons for the evident decline in the rate of suicides at that time which had dropped suddenly by one third between 1960 and 1970. Possible explanations for this trend were offered. The change from coal gas to the less toxic North Sea variety made the gas oven a less effective means of suicide. Pharmaceutical advances meant that drugs prescribed for depressive symptoms were less likely to be potentially lethal barbiturates than more modern tricyclics and other drugs which required a much higher dose to be fatal. In any case coroners frequently gave open verdicts in order to protect the families. The other major factor, and the one firmly backed by Fox, was the rapid growth in the number of Samaritan branches during that period. In a paper given to the World Health Organisation in 1974 he compared numbers of calls to The Samaritans in 1964, when records were first kept, (12,000) with 1973 (156,00). He acknowledged that the similar figures for 1971 might have been artificially boosted by the transmission of the TV series, *The Befrienders*, which had a successful run that year, as well as the launching of two new initiatives, the Festival branch aimed at young callers and the Correspondence branch, based in Scotland and designed to appeal to those who were particularly isolated.

Fox then went on to talk of the research by sociologist Christopher Bagley in the late 60s in which he studied 30 towns. 15 of these had had Samaritan branches since 1962; the other 15, with similar characteristics had no branch. His results appeared startlingly dramatic. Those towns with a branch had seen the suicide rate in their catchments drop by 5.8 per cent while their parallel towns had seen a rise of 19.8 per cent. This appeared to prove statistically that the service was having a marked effect. Subsequent research by Barraclough et al. undermined these results, as it proved impossible to replicate the experiment, an essential for scientific proof to be accepted. Bagley, writing in the *Lancet* in 1978, ten years after his initial project acknowledged that his research was flawed, coming to the conclusion that it would never be possible to evaluate fully the impact of any particular branch or the organisation as a whole since a branch with good location or availability might have an effect on a neighbouring area. A centre in Leicester for example might have an influence on the population of Nottingham. Sometimes geography can impact in a negative way. This might apply to centres such as Shetland, where it could be difficult for a local resident to go to the Lerwick centre anonymously, but they might be happy to talk to, say, Aberdeen.

Bagley concluded his article by saying, *"Samaritans may be effective in reducing suicide rates to some extent, but there is no way of proving this...What is incontrovertible, I think is that The Samaritans provides an invaluable counselling service for those in distress."*

Though volunteers would not call themselves *counsellors* as this implies that they try to reconstruct people's lives rather than befriend and support them, this kind of acceptance by professionals is an encouragement. The only kind of proof is always going to have to rely on the fact that callers go on increasing year by year and many of them return many times for help.

There are occasions when someone does come back to say thanks. Christmas time usually brings a crop of cards from grateful callers and sometimes a letter is received which makes volunteers feel that it is all worthwhile as the following extract from a letter received in September 2000 shows (disguised to protect the caller's identity):

"I want to thank you with all my heart for being there. When I made the phone call and was not able to speak because my throat was choked I heard a voice say 'it's all right, take your time. This line is for you.' I felt it was the first time in my life that there was something there just for me and gradually I was able to speak to her, hesitantly while

she kept saying 'there's no hurry' and as I went on I could feel my stomach calming and I was able to pick up what she was saying to me in response to my confusion...I felt I could tell her anything ... I did not have to feel guilty. Somehow in the things she said I began to feel that I could become part of the world and maybe I might be able to survive even though I am so alone (I am not really alone,

Elizabeth Pearce, director of Belfast, launches a publicity campaign

I have a husband and family)...Thank you so much."

Less common are the occasions like the one when a Rolls Royce drew up outside one Saturday disgorging a uniformed chauffeur clutching a huge bouquet of flowers for the volunteer who had the previous week *"helped my mistress"*.

For most individual volunteers a thank you is not required. There are many very moving calls from people whose distress is such that the listener feels thankful that he or she was there, if only, as in many cases, as a sounding board. No organisation worth its salt should be complacent about its performance, since self-evaluation may be the most effective, way of keeping up the standards. Within The Samaritans there has been, since the mid-60s, a system for helping branches to look at their own performance. In the early days branches would be visited by members of the executive, but soon a panel of branch visitors was set up. These were volunteers with some experience of running a branch, usually though not always as director, who would go in pairs to individual branches. As time went on the panel became more formalised and visitors themselves were carefully selected and trained for their work. Nobody can do a branch visit unless they have attended a training school in the previous twelve months and, since 2001, no visitor can remain on the panel if they have not been a member of the Council of Management in the last six years. The introduction of this rule was sudden and caused heartache amongst some.

Besides the evaluation of individual branches, there have been periods of national navel-gazing. In 1977 Mike Charman put a paper to the national conference in which he posed a number of important questions:

"Have we forgotten the needs of the client? Are we becoming too professional? Are we so fond of success and assisting clients that we are losing the suicidal and despairing because we think we know it all?"

As long as such questions can be addressed, an organisation will remain healthy.

The 100th Samaritan *cover*

Out of the brown paper bag

1. Anonymity

For the first couple of decades of Samaritan work it was accepted by everyone that to tell one's friends that one was a volunteer was a betrayal of the organisation. Received wisdom dictated that if anyone knew who the Samaritans were, they would be discouraged from calling. There may have been cases where this a was so, but later experiences have shown that it was a misconception. One branch, celebrating its 25th anniversary, wanted to order a cake but was so concerned about anonymity that it would not ask for the word *Samaritan* to be included in the iced message on top.

Even nowadays there are areas where anonymity is a major issue. These include small, geographically circumscribed areas such as the island branches of which there are currently seven. Some volunteers find it well-nigh impossible even to put up a poster for fear of being *outed* as a Samaritan. One pair of island volunteers coming over on the boat together to a conference tell of their embarrassment when, laden with overnight bags, they encountered a close colleague of the lady Samaritan's husband who looked extremely askance, not to say very curious, at seeing her in the company of a much younger, rather handsome male, obviously off for some kind of weekend assignation. This is a similar experience to that of many a female volunteer being dropped off at home at 7.30 am by a strange man after an overnight duty, subjected to the close scrutiny of inquisitive neighbours. A volunteer from a Scottish branch who feared she had been spotted giving a Samaritan talk in public confessed to her friends where she had been and why. *"Oh, thank God"* was the reply, *"we thought you were having an affair!"* Another volunteer was overheard at a national conference to tell everyone that she had *"given talks to every agency in her village, and the surrounding area"*. Later on she declared that *"she had kept herself anonymous"* all the years she had been in the branch. The incredulous reaction of her audience brought her up short as the penny dropped. *"Oh! Of course everyone knows I'm a Samaritan, from my talks!"*

In 1971 the bright yellow newsletter sent out to branches from the general office at Slough, ruled out firmly the possibility of car-stickers on the grounds that potential callers, seeing the notices, might lie in wait for a Samaritan to come back to the car. It went on to point out the dire consequences if the owner was not a volunteer but merely a supporter. *"The director"*, it said, *"must be known, to gain public confidence. Otherwise Samaritans are anonymous at all times and in all places."*

Gradually the perception began to change. There had always been high profile members who did not appear to be affecting the caller rate adversely so why should local volunteers not appear in public? It began to be joked that volunteers went around with a brown paper bag over their heads.

In 1978 the whole topic of anonymity was discussed by the Council of Management and its Executive Committee. Doris, the life president was quite clear that there were three different levels of self-revelation to the public. The easiest to resolve was the need to present Samaritan work in the community. In many localities the identities of those volunteers working with other agencies or individuals were habitually cloaked in secrecy. This became untenable as working outside the branch became more common. How could a Samaritan give only first name and number when working with professionals. Eglantine 666 would stand out like a sore thumb amongst Rev. Jack Bloggs, Superintendent Dave Soap or Mary Wotsit from the Council for Voluntary Service. In any case, as the then chairman, Michael Yorke, pointed out, professionals would find it difficult to believe that they could not be trusted with the full name of the member with whom they were working.

Much more frowned upon was the use of one's membership to further one's own prestige. Even now, a volunteer would not be expected to boast about his or her membership. There was a rather grey area here, though. What if a volunteer applied for a job or position and wished to mention membership of the organisation as part of the application? It was recognised by some, including the chairman, that there might be occasions where this could be appropriate, where the membership was directly relevant to the post. Doris' third category was *idle chatter*, always to be abhorred.

In 1985, writing in the *Samaritan* magazine, Chad himself restated the principle of anonymity. He was answering a non-Samaritan speaker at the York conference who had suggested that volunteers should *come out of the closet*. Chad took exception to this terminology, pointing out that it was normally used in connection with homosexuals. He had always agreed that those who needed to be known by name should be, and he dismissed any idea of an *anonymous* publicity officer, for example, but he was convinced that it was unacceptable to use one's membership for personal reasons. One volunteer had, in fact, he rejoiced, been asked to leave because he tried to use his membership to gain him votes in a local election.

Ordinary volunteers sometimes found breaches of their cover somewhat inconvenient. Mary, of Watford, (now South West Herts) writing in the same edition, remembered being accosted in a supermarket by a rather formidable representative of a group to whom Mary had been speaking recently stressing the fact that Samaritans are *ordinary* people. The lady cast a regal eye over the toilet rolls and similarly mundane contents of the trolley and said, *"well I can see, you really are ordinary"*. On a more embarrassing occasion, she was walking up the High Street with her mother-in-law when their eyes lighted upon a group of alcoholics. Ma-in-law was just beginning to comment on their presence when one broke away from his group, reeled across the pavement and shouted, *"Look boys! It's my darling Mary!"* He'd visited the centre on her last shift.

Working in the open also brought its problems. A volunteer carrying out an official visit to the Festival branch was delighted that her brief was to be at the Glastonbury Festival to see how things were done. All went well until her attention was alerted by a loud cry of, *"Miss -, what are you doing here?"* A practising teacher, her cover was blown by one of her own students. Not that it was too serious - her street cred. went up enormously! There were also times when blown cover could be advantageous. A member of Festival branch discovered that the workers' bar behind the stage and the Samaritan tent at a particular festival was being run by colleagues from her work at a local court. Her cover was blown, but the drinks were extra cheap for the Samaritan team for the duration!

It is commonly recognised now, in the 21st century, that in fact it can be a very positive feature of Samaritan work. Now that members more often have a face, there is a definite advantage for recruitment. A large number of current volunteers, possibly a majority, have been influenced by members in their decision to apply.

Samaritans from Kirkcaldy and Edinburgh branches at the Royal Highland Show

2. Heads above the parapet

Festival branch

The beginning of this new approach stemmed initially from some concerns which arose about how little appeal The Samaritans seemed to have amongst the younger age-groups who were known to be high risk. Experience amongst student Nightlines which were fairly widespread in colleges and universities by the late 60s showed that there was much anxiety and stress amongst students, but suggested that these potential clients were not interested in the Samaritans. This prompted a number of young Samaritan volunteers, mainly based in Central London and Leicester to take a closer look at the problem. They first began to meet early in 1972 and spent much time exploring ideas on how to approach young people, especially those with less than conventional life-styles. This has to be seen in the context of the huge changes in social behaviour which had begun in the *Swinging 60s* and continued into the 70s. The pop scene and the drug culture which now dominated the younger age-groups meant a special kind of awareness was required. Out of these discussions eventually emerged a whole new concept of Samaritan work - the idea of offering the service outside the branches. Dick Blackwell, who was to become the first director of the Festival branch put the point, *"if they won't come to us, we'd better go to them"*.

It's not always fun for everybody, if that's the way it is with you, look out for the samaritans

The first sign of this was the appearance of a small Samaritan tent at a pop festival at Bardney, near Lincoln. A handful of willing volunteers and some from the Nightlines spent the duration of the festival befriending around

Festival branch is 21 years old (1993)

30 distressed people, while the likes of Joe Cocker did their stuff on stage. Later in the same year, two volunteers worked with other welfare groups at the Windsor Free Festival. In the autumn of 1972 the Pop Festival Project was recognised as an experimental project. In the following year, work at the Trentishoe (Devon), Buxton and Reading festivals amply demonstrated the need for this kind of service and so the Festival branch of The Samaritans, number 149, was born on 1 June 1974.

This was an enormous change in the Samaritan approach and it could hardly be foreseen at the time of its inception how far-reaching an effect it would have. From the Festival branch which was and still is a very specialised part of the work which would not suit every volunteer, came befriending in the open, (BITO) a development of the Samaritan service which was carried out by a wide range of people right across the movement (though not without some special preparation for the work). This was supported by the arrival of Arnold, a converted coach which the Festival branch shared with the rest of the movement so that by the late 80s the whole concept of working outside the branch had evolved into a wide-ranging programme of reaching out to particularly vulnerable groups in the community.

The Festival branch has continued to be unique, being the only non-brick face to-face branch in the movement. (The other non-brick branch is the Samaritan Correspondence branch which responds only by letter.) The Festival team works in a very different way from other volunteers in the sense that they have to give their services over very short but intensive periods. In between there are substantial gaps, since festivals tend to be in the summer months. In the winter there are other opportunities for Festival volunteers, such as a presence in Trafalgar Square over New Year. The work is carried out from a tent (or several) and continues throughout the day and night. Working in an open situation leaves the volunteers much more vulnerable than in the security of a centre, so there is a particularly strong sense of support both between volunteers and from the leaders in charge of shifts. Volunteers crash out for short spells of sleep in between shifts and feed themselves from a sort of field-kitchen. It has often been joked that in more conventional branches volunteers are obsessed by discussing demanding callers. In the festival scene it is the state of the lavatories which provides the topic of conversation. Nowadays a great pop festival would not be the same without the huge orange (now green) Samaritan banners and pennants though it took a little time for the punters to become accustomed to them. At the Reading Festival in 1983 the following remarks from passers-by were noted:

- *It must be quite strange, sitting there looking approachable.*
- *They're not REAL Samaritans are they?*
- *Oh look, there's the Samaritans. Now we'll go to the Salvation Army, their beds are more comfortable.*
- *Samaritans - are they the ones with the friendly ears?*
- *You can't be a Samaritan. You look too much like a punter.*
- *Hello there. Can you help me? I'm a reincarnated lemming.*
- *Is it true the Samaritans don't drink?*

(Just for the record, the answer to this last is *"no"*!)

These comments were passed on by Rex who has given the movement a huge amount over the years, not only as one of the longest serving (and, dare it be said, oldest) members of the Festival branch but also as the national publicity officer and a member of the team who worked on reaching out to older people in the late 80s and early 90s. He has always been a great character, instantly recognisable from the fact that he invariably appeared at Samaritan functions barefoot. It used to be assumed by the stick-in-the-muds from brick branches that no shoes, long hair, flowing garments (female) and earrings (male) were clearly identifiable badges of Festival members.

"Way back in the mid to late 70s...whilst doing my afternoon shifts at CLB, I was enticed by reports of this new branch..which went to pop festivals and worked in the open air. Having recently been a punter myself at a Knebworth…and seen someone behaving in an extremely disturbed manner and needing some form of help, I decided I'd have a go at joining this new branch….I was invited to a selection meeting in a hall somewhere

near Uxbridge. I entered a large room where about forty people of varying descriptions had gathered and we all sat round the wall in a large circle. It...became...obvious in a short time that no one was going to take the lead and we didn't know who was already a member...Eventually it became obvious that the person in some form of responsibility was Dick Blackwell who then became the target for questions, roughly along the lines of what the hell is this all about?...By lunchtime we went to the pub...and I palled up with a guy called Graham, a good mate to this day. After seriously debating whether to stay in the pub or go back we eventually attended the afternoon small group sessions...To this day I have no idea how we were selected.

Anyway, I'm glad we were and three of us from that meeting are still in the branch...We have always had...full weekend (meetings) at a location from where it is difficult to escape...We always used to go in for a great deal of navel gazing. I used to hate those weekends. I always felt that I was the only one who wasn't a social worker, who didn't smoke...and, even worse, the only one who enjoyed eating meat."

This volunteer goes on to describe how the branch went in for delving into their innermost psyches with a view to making them better volunteers. Festival branch was not alone in this. During the early 80s it was felt that proper empathetic responses to a caller could not be achieved without complete self-awareness regarding one's attitude to dying and suicide. This emphasis has moderated considerably since then. There were for many great difficulties in delving in this way. As Richard says *"for someone in their early twenties, lucky enough to have a job...doing a higher degree, having a lovely girlfriend...and even an open top car and a motor bike...analysing the deepest recesses of one's psyche (was) rather difficult and I felt like making up problems just to be one of the crowd."* He was certainly not alone in this feeling and it was not the subject of great regret when training schools and the like shifted their emphasis.

Festival training was not all gloom, however. Another volunteer recalls that weekend sessions at Stoneleigh could charge the volunteers' batteries. *"It always had a warm and welcoming atmosphere, even when we knew we were to spend part of the weekend out in the cold, role-playing a festival with all its many different callers played by Festival branch volunteers determined to do their best to test...skills to the full.*

Sometimes laughter just got the better of us watching Trevor or Graham playing the drunk caller (rather too well we mostly thought) but mainly we were lost in the atmosphere of it all...The best role plays...were to be found...when we were highlighting the difficulties of thorny issues and the desperate callers who so often came to us at all hours...The bulk of the people we saw were young, lost and sad - sometimes out of their depth in the frightening atmosphere of a festival which was larger and wetter and colder than they had reckoned on."

Festival branch attended three main festivals in 1974 and befriended 93 callers. In 1999, its 25th anniversary year, 15 pop and rock festivals were attended and 3,915 callers were helped. Besides all this the branch was, and still is, involved in the New Year celebrations and the Crisis at Christmas project. It still helps with events in other places where local branches are also involved.

3. Arnold and friends

The new volunteer who appeared on the scene in 1978 to help the work in the open air was a rather elderly single-decker coach with the registration number ARN 775C, hence his anthropomorphic title. The idea was that the coach would provide facilities for a mobile centre, not just for use at festivals but in other contexts too. The money to purchase and convert the vehicle came from the Carnegie Trust, and Arnold soon appeared resplendent in orange Samaritan livery and with posters along the sides. Inside there were areas for working in, somewhere to allow volunteers to sleep, and an area which could be screened off for confidential interviews.

This opened up new possibilities, of going outside brick branches to recruit, to spread publicity, or to fund-raise as well as offering traditional Samaritan help. All those who were to work with the bus were given special awareness raising sessions. The most important messages were to look approachable at all times and to look out for the shy caller who would not approach willingly but would rather lurk at a distance hoping to be approached by the volunteer. This presented a whole new departure for many non-Festival volunteers. It was fairly unheard of to be so pro-active. Any work done outside the branch before had always been at the express request of the caller. Now it was up to those on duty. The idea of Arnold being a member of the volunteer force was perpetuated by the style of report on his activities adopted by his *Mum*, Norah from Portsmouth, who had taken over his management team in 1981. Writing in the magazine in the winter edition of 1982-3 she wrote the article in the form of a letter.

Dear Samaritans,

I thought you might like to know how I have been getting on this year, but first of all, I want to thank you for my major overhaul. I feel so much better and years younger, even my drivers think so as I don't hear awful words when they are driving me round…Do you know I went to the South of England, Essex, Salisbury, Kent show, etc.

The letter goes on to list other visits that year, including the Farnborough Air Show and the international IFOTES conference in York, where it was suggested that a visit might be paid to Singapore. (This was wishful thinking as the costs would have been prohibitive.)

I really enjoyed the AGM in September, that was because so many of you came to visit me...I do hope you went back to your branches and told them how useful I can be, and though lots of you think I'm just a publicity person, I know I'm not cos I've read the reports on me and how many people came to talk to me (and you)...I KNOW that lots of them found it easier talking to me in the open.

I've just thought of something. I'm the only Samaritan who doesn't have to be anonymous. You spend so much time making sure no-one recognises you, and I want everyone to know me. Poor you, lucky me.

Lots of love,

Arnold.

This rather whimsical approach, which might not have been to everyone's taste, was deliberate as it certainly drew attention to a whole new culture in the service. For many, the anonymity issue created real problems and volunteers were often known to travel to neighbouring towns to help out rather than being visible in their own. Mandy from Lewisham, writing in the magazine about her first ever appearance in the open (at least as a Samaritan) said,

"'What the hell are you doing amongst this group of weirdos?' Such was the sentiment of one of the visitors to the Festival of Mind, Body and Spirit at Olympia. I must admit I had thoughts in that direction myself at first. Our stand had been organised by Festival branch, though many of the volunteers there were, like me, regular branch Samaritans doing this for the first time...I felt somewhat confused as to our precise role at the festival. I was clutching a handful of leaflets but was not sure if we were supposed to thrust them at unsuspecting passers-by or those who seemed to be hovering uncertainly...Eventually, I became accustomed to approaching people...many said they'd been wondering how to join us. Two girls, after talking for a while asked, Can normal people join?...

The final word should come from the two young men I heard as I was leaving my shift. 'Hey,' said the first, 'the Samaritans, what are they selling?' 'Suicide, man,' replied his friend. 'Far out!'"

The work of Festival branch and Arnold resulted in an explosion of activity throughout the Samaritan world. Regions and branches began to acquire their own equipment for working outside. Tents, trailers, caravans, retired ambulances and even private cars were pressed into service and it was not long before orange and black Samaritan banners were a familiar sight at country fairs, agricultural and flower shows, on village greens and in town centres.

All this activity was not without hazard, however, and many a BITO volunteer can tell of tents demolished in torrential rainstorms, of shows where flash floods swept into the car park up to neck-height and even one famous occasion, in Bury, Lancs, when a horse, spooked by a sudden noise, swerved violently and dragged its cart right into, and through the Samaritan stall, taking volunteer, Stephen, with it. Fortunately he lived to tell the tale, and at least the branch received some free publicity in the local press! A stand set up by the York volunteers was apparently in a prime spot - until they noticed the word EXIT right above their heads!

Arnold was eventually retired and replaced by a purpose-built mobile centre named *Dennis* after his designer, John Dennis of Dennis fire engines. This vehicle travelled far and wide, continuing the work in the open.

A smaller, easier to use *Promobile* joined the team in 1990. This was intended mainly for publicity purposes and was available for use by any branch prepared to look after it properly. It could only be driven by a holder of a PSV licence which sometimes led to problems of handing over from one branch to the next. Its health was looked after by Bryn from Cardiff, originally one of Dennis' drivers who could often be found driving it long distances up and down the country. It even visited some of the outlying island branches. The management of the vehicles was passed to Peter Newman of Northampton in 1990.

Vehicles were not always as great to use as their owners hoped. As Arnold mentioned, servicing and repair work could be an important item. Many an ex-

ambulance or similar found itself marooned in some inconvenient spot having broken down. This could occasionally be a bonus as it was once in Wakefield when the vehicle, complete with all its posters and displays, broke down in the middle of a busy bridge. It was stuck there all day, in a prime site for high-profile publicity.

4. Outreach

In the mid-80s much thought was given to a new approach to those people who were recognised statistically to be at risk of suicide and, it was felt, could benefit from Samaritan help, but who did not make contact. Groups were identified to whom particular approaches might be made. Besides the work being done in the open, young people, elderly people, those in prison, those in hospital, residents in rural areas, particularly farmers, ethnic minorities and those involved in major disasters were given top priority, and co-ordinators were appointed to develop these projects. In 1990 a national outreach officer in the enthusiastic person of Di Stubbs was appointed to the general office staff.

Di Stubbs

The need for this extension to the work was quite clearly shown by research. Tables of suicide figures placed different groups in order of their suicide risks. Doctors, farmers and vets came very high but even so it was sometimes difficult to tempt volunteers out of their branches. In some cases this was the result of a purely practical problem, lack of resources. Naturally branch directors were very concerned about ensuring that their duty rotas were covered so they could not envisage sending volunteers to work outside. In fact this was an early misinterpretation of the outreach projects. What was required was the building of bridges with other organisations and with groups in the community. It was not necessarily expected that a group of volunteers should set up shop in the local hospital for example, though many did, with excellent results. Equally important though was the work done with the professions, for example, making them aware of the signs of suicide risk and the nature of the service offered on which they could call for help for their patients or clients. A leaflet entitled *You are the link* was produced for circulation to these professionals, explaining how to work together. As time went on some of the problems became clear. There were groups which were particularly hard to reach, young people, whose perception of the middle-aged, middle-class Samaritan has yet to be broken despite the great efforts by the national youth officers, Dick Blackwell, Anthony Lawton, Peter Eldrid and Nick Ellerby each of whom produced materials for use in schools and youth organisations starting as early as the late 1960s.

The Youth Communication Project designed by Anthony Lawton was published around 1979 and was circulated to schools for use with students. It

contained a wealth of information about suicide, the Samaritans and the kinds of problems which might confront young people. There were fictitious case-studies and material for inter-active work. This was a pioneering piece of work at the time and was the forerunner to much work at both local and national levels in schools and colleges. Sadly this is an area which constantly needs to be updated since youth culture moves on so quickly. A film which was produced for school use was, when it came out bang up to the minute, but within a very few years, students began to find the appearance, language and behaviour of the protagonists more amusing than helpful, so the message was lost.

The work in schools and colleges goes on, though the days of the youth officer, and later the co-ordinator for work with young people (the last of these, Alison Weisselberg finished her term in 2000), are now past. Young men are still of great concern, having a very high rate of suicide and a low contact record. New ways are always being sought to overcome the barriers including working with other agencies in order to offer support to this group, as the Manchester branch, for example, works with the initiative known as CALM (Campaign Against Living Miserably), specifically aimed at young men.

Placing publicity materials and talking to groups of people was relatively easy in these areas, but a further attempt to reach potential callers, those of different ethnic origin, proved more difficult. It soon became clear to the first co-ordinator, Pat from Enfield branch, that the volunteers themselves were the

Early outreach co-ordinators. From the left, Bob Arrowsmith, Events; Kathy Biggar, Prisons; Pat Crew, Transcultural; Janet Pugh, Rural; Chris Hall, Hospitals; Steve Beswick, Youth; Ken Hall, Disasters and Ben Finny, Older People

ones who needed to be educated, not because they were in any way unaccepting of callers of other ethnic backgrounds, but they were often unaware of some of the sensitivities that different groups might have. Her work and that of Leeyah from Cheltenham, her successor, helped to create a new awareness, though much remains to be done. Similarly, work carried out by Les (Bournemouth) on gender and sexual orientation issues revealed a need for education within the organisation.

Another group of people who were, and still are, hard to reach were those of more mature years. Suicide statistics show constantly that there is a serious risk of suicide especially for men over 70. There is no doubt that many older people become very depressed and this may be dismissed by their nearest and dearest as *typical Granny*, but with help it could be alleviated. There are a number of barriers here, however. Factors such as pride, fear, physical incapacity, reluctance to talk about private matters can all inhibit contact. For this reason a national team led by Ben Finny was set up to try to develop strategies for reaching these people. Paper napkins with the Samaritan message on were sent

An example of a joint initiative, Stafford branch. This kind of card would be issued to individuals or groups working with older people. It points out clearly the difference in the two types of service, the one practical, the other supportive and confidential. Several branches made similar arrangements

to Meals on Wheels organisers and Samaritans made appearances at exhibitions catering for elderly or disabled people. At local level contact with medical professionals and carers' groups was encouraged. Pat from Banbury did much to link Samaritans with the carers' organisations.

Even more difficult to reach was, and still is, the rural community. Farmers have a very high suicide rate but are very reluctant to seek help. To compound the problem, they also have access to a violent

means of death, since guns are commonly found on farms. The liaison by Janet Pugh with a wide range of rural groups on a county by county basis led to the setting up of rural outreach programmes in conjunction with the CAB who could help with practical problems and advice while The Samaritans offered emotional support. Cards containing the details of how and where to make contact were widely distributed. More recently, during the disastrous foot and mouth epidemic of 2001, a sustained campaign of television advertising, which

Richard Kerkham, national co-ordinator for work in rural areas in the late 1990s

many people found very powerful, and a booklet issued to many rural destinations were designed to open doors for those suffering from the tragedy. Work in hospitals was also initiated at this time. Sometimes a room would be allocated for Samaritan use so that volunteers would be available at certain times in the week. It was hoped that this would help patients who were feeling particularly low or suicidal. It was also recognised that doctors were one of the groups with a high risk of suicide, so it was hoped to reach the professionals as well as the patients. In the same way, work in prisons was aimed at making contact at every level with those *inside*. This work became the great success of the reaching out programme and has now been incorporated into the mainstream caller care work in the branches.

One important part of outreach is disaster planning. A number of serious incidents in which many were hurt prompted the setting up of a national team to help in any way they could. It was realised fairly early on, after involvement in the Kegworth air crash and other incidents, that the best help Samaritans could offer was as the back-up to the major services. It would not be helpful to get in their way while the operation was in progress, but it would be a valuable source of help in the aftermath of a disaster both for victims and their families and for the helpers too.

Every branch was encouraged to draw up a disaster plan with instructions as to how to proceed in the event of a disaster. Liaison with the disaster planning committees in each area would ensure that the Samaritan input was as helpful as possible. A booklet by Ken Hall who was the first disaster co-ordinator gave full information as to how to proceed. Ken is now well known to all conference goers as *the bookstall man*.

From its inception under the title of *outreach* in about 1986, through to the end of the 90s, during which time it had become known as *reaching out*, the progress of the various projects was monitored. New approaches were made to carers, to the armed forces, originally by Anna of Ashford and later Liz, formerly of Swindon, now of Plymouth. Text phones for callers with hearing difficulties were also installed.

One enduring project has been work with the homeless (by Len of Teesside and Fredwyn of Enfield Haringey Barnet). This group is one of the most vulnerable and one of the most elusive. It also includes many young people, as well as many with psychiatric problems. Various projects have been run, including offering free phone cards so that people could ring Samaritans. Co-operation with the *Big Issue* sellers has also been tried. Those with a history of attempting suicide and those with dependencies (by Bill of CLB) have also been targeted. The area of disability was studied by Leon of Bournemouth who soon realised that it was branches themselves who needed to be educated about accessibility and other important related issues. His work, with the support of his wife, Bridget and others like Beris from Sheffield has achieved a much greater understanding of the whole issue.

At the time of writing the various aspects of reaching out have been under review as part of the *Facing the future* evaluation of what is being done at present, leading to a *re-branding* for the 21st century. It remains to be seen where it will go from here.

Outside looking in - prisons

One of the most remarkable developments in Samaritan work over the last twenty or so years has been the evolution of its work in prisons. This originally belonged to the general area of *outreach* which was aimed at those groups most at risk but who were not asking for help. In the case of people on remand or serving custodial sentences, they were not only amongst those most likely to kill themselves, but were also, being behind bars, unable to make any contact. Some local branches began to try to make contact with their local prisons, but with minimal success. It gradually became clear to some of those who had been involved in outreach for some time, like Kathy Biggar, who also had experience of working in a local prison, that the only way forward was to take a national perspective. In 1986 The Samaritans were approached by the then Director of Prison Medical Services to look at the possibility of some joint initiative as a part of his review of the Prison Service in England and Wales' policy regarding the suicidal in custody. Discussions about the possibility of support for both prisoners and staff took place, laying a foundation for future work. At local level, the positive role of a nearby branch in offering befriending was gradually acknowledged.

In 1989 the then Inspector of Prisons, Judge Stephen Tumin took a very clear stand in his recommendations on the possible role of The Samaritans in prisons and this, combined with the attitude of the Prison Medical Services, led to the formation of a partnership with the Prison Service. Within a year a formal working relationship was formed with SASU, the Suicide Awareness Support Unit of the Prison Service. Between 1991 and 1994 Kathy Biggar, whose professional experience eminently qualified her for the role, was seconded to work with The Samaritans and with SASU to further the relationship between HM Prison Service and The Samaritans. This was a period of breakthrough, since many prisons at local level had in the first instance found the concept of allowing Samaritan volunteers inside to befriend prisoners difficult to accept. Once the idea had national and official backing, things became easier. This was achieved by a combination of encouraging branches to become members of the prisons' suicide awareness or prevention teams, building up links with prisons by phone, by visiting and by offering a befriending service on the wings. Many prisons welcomed the Samaritan presence once the links were established and in many cases would have been pleased to have volunteers on hand every day of the week. Sadly, most branches did not have the resources for this kind of operation, and in some areas, prison befriending put a great strain on volunteer resources. A national training package for those working in prisons was produced and local training was provided. A team of six provided support on a regional basis though each one had to cover a huge area.

The experience of prison work for many volunteers was quite different from any other part of the work. The actual feeling of being *inside* could be quite daunting: the clanging of gates, rattling of keys and the distinctive smell all contributed to the claustrophobic effect. In some places an officer would lock new volunteers into a cell so that they could get the feel of what it was like for the residents. A new group, approaching their prison for the first time, nervously asked the officer in charge of the gate, *"Samaritans. May we come in?"* was told, *"We let any bugger in, it's the getting out that's the problem!"*

Having said this, the work proved very rewarding. In some places, volunteers were allocated a room where befriending could be done in confidence while in others the practice was for them to be available on the wings, usually during the *free-association* (leisure) time of the prisoners. Sometimes the officers on duty would suggest that the volunteers go and see someone in their own cell, especially if they were particularly down. The VPU (Vulnerable Prisoners Unit) where many of those most at risk were often to be found was also visited as well as the hospital wing. Experiences varied from place to place, but for many volunteers the contacts they had with suicidal or severely depressed prisoners were some of the most touching and emotionally draining of the whole of their Samaritan careers.

For some time a watching brief had been kept on work being done in the States, specifically in Charles Street Jail in Boston, Mass. where the Samaritan branch had involved prisoners in offering support to their fellows in the early 80s. The success of the project which proved that Samaritan principles could be adapted to the prison setting, resulted in a pilot scheme being set up in Swansea prison in July 1991. From there, the idea began to spread, and with the new strategy launched in 1994 by the Prison Service under the title of *Caring for the Suicidal in Custody*, Samaritan involvement was consolidated and prisoner participation encouraged.

One of the biggest issues which had to be resolved, was that of confidentiality. In all Samaritan work this principle is absolute and there was no way in which it could be compromised because of the unusual circumstances. For some in the Prison service this was unacceptable, especially when Samaritans might only be in the prison once a week for a couple of hours. The question was asked whether those who had responsibility for the inmates should be told if one of them was suicidal. Once Listener schemes were in place, where prisoners were selected carefully and trained in listening skills in order to offer support to their fellows in distress, this matter had to be finalised. It is now firmly established, and accepted by all, that all befriending in a prison context is confidential. Had it not been so, the credibility of the whole scheme would have come into question.

Once Kathy's secondment as a professional came to an end, a volunteer national prison support co-ordinator was appointed. By 1995 the work in prisons had became part of mainstream caller-care work in the branches instead of a separate reaching out activity. The work of Paul Rubinstein, Sheila Coggrave and Ann Nicholl successively continued the process of building the relationship between the prison service and The Samaritans, and there were 70 Listener befriending schemes in England and Wales and one in Scotland. By this time all prison establishments in England and Wales and some in Northern Ireland, Scotland and Eire, were ensuring that all prisoners could

The Prison Support Team in Swansea, August 1993. The prison governor, Jim Heyes with Kathy Biggar and Paul Rubinstein. Other members shown are Aidan from Cork, Eileen from Warrington, Jan from Bath, Jean from Nottingham, Joyce from Swansea, Margaret from Guildford and Stanley from Perth

have the opportunity to contact the local branch in the case of severe crisis at any time of the day or night.

In 1996 the first joint Samaritan-Prison Service-Listener conference was organised. This has become an annual event with the full participation of the most important members of the Prison Service, including the Director General of Prisons who always attends.

Around this time the emphasis for volunteers began to change. Key

Samaritans and Listeners in Wandsworth. Chad with Merg of Putney to his left and Kathy of CLB and Kit of Putney to his right

responsibilities for branches were now the selecting and training of prisoners to be Listeners, setting up and attending regular support meetings where Listeners can share their feelings and ensuring that Listeners can have 24 hour access by phone to their local branch. A talk by Sheila Coggrave in 1997 at Lilleshall did much to convince prison staff of the vital importance of confidentiality, always somewhat of a stumbling block before this.

Since 1997 much has been achieved. The up-dating of *The guide to befriending in prisons* and the consolidation of methods for selection and training of Listeners clarified the role of branches and every prison received a prison service order, *the role of The Samaritans* setting the official seal on the work.

Listeners are now allowed to attend Samaritan conferences in order to give presentations about their work. On one emotional occasion, a Listener from Askham Grange prison which is close to York gave such a moving account of how she felt about the work that she was given a standing ovation. This made her break down in tears saying, *"This is the first time I've felt as if I was being treated as a human being in the past eight years."* Many Listeners have felt their whole life change for the better because of being allowed to help others. It can give them a sense of self worth which they have, in some cases, never felt before.

Les Lavender, former Governor of HMP Nottingham represented the view of many of his colleagues in the Prison Service when he wrote, *"There can be very few better ways of illustrating our respect for human dignity than to provide opportunities for those in distress to have an empathetic ear and to give those who provide the ear the credit and respect they have merited."* Research on the re-offending rates of those who have been Listeners is expected to show a considerable drop and some ex-prisoners have already been accepted as Samaritan volunteers on their release.

The work on suicide in prisons goes on developing. The Chief Inspector of Prisons thematic review entitled *Suicide is everyone's concern* was published in 1999 and in 2000 a report recommended that prisons should be categorised according to their need. This led to the launch of the Risk One Project. Its report, issued in 2001 recommended that all prisons should focus on the enabling of Listener schemes backed by Samaritan training and support.

The Suicide Awareness Unit is now the Safer Custody Group, reflecting a slight shift of emphasis away from simple awareness to a more focused effort to prevent suicide.

In 2002 there were 117 Listener schemes in England and Wales, nine in Scotland and three in embryo in Eire, and it seems likely that the number will continue to grow.

Reaching dark corners

Once the movement became fully established, it was soon recognised that there were potential callers who were simply not getting in touch. This led to thoughts about how to work beyond the brick confines of branches. Festival branch broke the mould by trying to make contact with young people through their own culture and attempts were beginning to be made to reach other groups. One concern was about the many households which had not had their own telephone for long, or did not have one at all, for whom the phone was only a bearer of bad news, not a means of personal communication. In order to reach these people, the Scottish correspondence branch was born. This had no brick centre, only a PO box number based in Stirling. David Arthur, not content with being a driving force in bringing Samaritans to Scotland in the first place, was a prime mover in setting up this new departure. Befriending by letter requires some specialised skills, since, unlike a verbal conversation which may be soon forgotten, anything written down has the potential to last for ever. A letter may be read and reread by its recipient. It is therefore essential that every word be carefully weighed. Nuances of meaning which may be conveyed by tone of voice, need special care on paper.

The branch received recognition as a full branch in 1972 and it provided the opportunity not only for new callers to make contact, but also for a new group of volunteers, such as those in remote areas, to contribute to the work.

The new Correspondence branch which combines the original branch with an extended team drawn from other parts of Britain was established in 1997.

Linking up

The historical development of the Samaritan movement created a structure in which each branch, though part of the whole, worked entirely independently of its neighbours. The technical impossibility of linking up telephones meant that each branch had its own phone number. Some of these, such as that in Manchester (BLA 9000), were chosen because of their similarity to the original MANsion House 9000 but others, though attempts were made to make them as memorable as possible, were quite different. In those days national publicity had to include the words *our number is in the book*. Nowadays we are quite used to the idea that national organisations, whether commercial or charitable, have a single number available anywhere, but in 1990 when this idea was first looked at for The Samaritans, it was much rarer.

At first there was some anxiety about the possibility of having only one number. Branches cherished, (and still do), their local identity which they feared might become subsumed into the anonymous whole. There were good reasons for trying, however. National advertising which included a single, simple method of contact seemed to offer improved availability. It was known that in many busy branches, the caller was likely to get an engaged tone, clearly giving the lie to the advertised promise that The Samaritans were always there. In some less busy branches there were lines free and volunteers were often under-employed. A single number would allow a caller to make immediate contact with a real person, clearly a good thing. Furthermore it would make better use of the volunteers' time and have the added advantage of retaining those who might otherwise have left because they felt they were wasting their time sitting by a phone which never rang. In the late 80s, Maurice Walton, then vice-chairman, had performed a mammoth task of mapping the areas covered by each branch, to show where their calls came from, where their volunteers lived, and, most important, where there were *black holes* not covered. It revealed that those who lived more than a local call's distance from their local branch were least likely to call, yet statistically it was known that these were the very people whose isolation might lead to despair and even suicide. The final advantage was that single number calls would only cost the local rate, however far away the caller.

Initially some volunteers found the idea intimidating and asked themselves how adequately they could befriend a caller from the other end of the country. Would a volunteer in Plymouth understand the accent of a caller from Aberdeen? Big city callers might find a volunteer from a remote rural area unable to comprehend the other's point of view. Problems of liaison between branches about caring for long-term callers, or following up calls were also widely expressed. How would the system work if an ambulance had to be called? Clearly there were some difficulties. It would be impossible, for example, to send out volunteers to help a caller from many miles away, (though in any case the use of the *flying squad* which used to be common in almost every branch had begun to decline substantially). Dare it be said that some worried about how other branches might treat *their* callers. These fears were soon laid to rest as it was realised that the kind of warmth and support which was being offered was universal and that the practical issues could soon be resolved by closer links between branches and regions.

The setting up of caller care teams in branches and regions, together with regional and national caller care co-ordination has been one of the most positive results of the system. Even the staunch enthusiasts were somewhat daunted by the risks of launching it all at once, so the Council of Management was advised to pilot it in Scotland first. This area was chosen partly because it was thought that the local advertising of a single number would be unlikely to *leak* into neighbouring regions. More importantly, it had the remotest areas and the scattered rural branches were underused compared to the great city branches in Glasgow and Edinburgh. It took many months of preparation but the new project was launched on 8 April 1991 using the number 0345 90 90 90.

The run up was not without its problems. Those working on the scheme from the Samaritan end had to fill in copious forms and make endless checks. Fortunately disaster was narrowly averted for one branch, Aberdeen, whose number had been recorded by British Telecom with one digit wrong. This would have meant their callers being put through to a butcher's shop in Chester. There was also no way of picking up changes of number, even if these originated from BT itself. Only four days before the Scottish launch, a routine test call made from a remote highland phone box was greeted by a recorded message which said, *"all Inverness numbers have been changed"*. Imagine the effect that might have had on a suicidal caller.

The launch of the single number in St Stephen's, 2 November 1995. Jenny Cunnington, then Chairman, standing, with HRH the Duchess of Kent, the Founder and Simon Armson

On the eve of the launch in Scotland, the BT engineers were struggling to perfect the scheme. The technology was still unable to cope with the fact that branches were taking calls both from the single number and their own local numbers. This meant that if a branch was engaged on its local number, the linkline call would not trip on to the next branch in the chain. This would negate the whole idea as the caller would get the engaged tone. This kind of problem meant that the full scheme could not be launched for another four and a half years. John Lawrie, who was responsible for the single number at the time, had to put forward eloquent arguments to persuade the increasingly frustrated Council of Management that everything possible was being done by the telephone technologists to iron out the problems. Eventually the good effects of the scheme became obvious and began to outweigh the difficulties so it was decided to launch the full scheme, now improved, if not perfect, on 2 November 1995, the 42nd birthday of the Samaritans, in the church of St Stephen Walbrook where it all began. The Royal Patron, HRH the Duchess of Kent made the first call.

The new technology was not cheap, and many volunteers had questioned the cost from the outset, being anxious that branches might be asked to contribute. It soon became obvious that the costs would fall sharply as the system became more widely used, but the initial cost seemed impossible to many. The launch was made possible through the generosity of WH Smith who made The Samaritans their chosen charity in their own bicentennial year and raised £1m towards the cost of the new system. This generosity was matched over the next few years by BT, who also gave £1m, the largest gift they had ever made to a single charity.

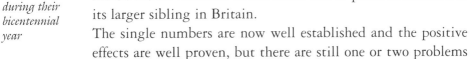

Sir Simon Hornby who was chairman of WH Smith during their bicentennial year

In Ireland it was the Government whose generosity made a similar system possible. At the end of his budget speech in 1991 the Irish Minister of Finance announced that Telecom Eireann, then owned by the Government, would waive all charges for special rate numbers for charities like The Samaritans. This allowed the link to be set up throughout the Republic though sadly as there are no links between the systems in the north and in the south the number has to be different. It could soon be seen that 1850 60 90 90 which linked the 12 branches in the south was to prove as effective as its larger sibling in Britain.

The single numbers are now well established and the positive effects are well proven, but there are still one or two problems of distribution. Large, busy branches have sometimes complained that their call rate has declined severely, while quiet branches, used to long periods of silence, have found themselves being deprived of sleep (which no city volunteer would expect), and on constant calls. Constant tweaking of the system still has to be carried out. The one remaining issue of concern to many is whether there will be a move to abolish local numbers. For many branches, who depend on their local identity for funds, grants and volunteers, this could be disastrous, despite the fact that the single number could now be expected to cope with all calls. It would perhaps be a pity if the organisation chose to lose the user-friendly connections with localities by creating one faceless centralised entity.

The white heat of technology

At the same time as the single number was being piloted, a new and exciting area was opening up. The development of the internet and e-mail presented a challenge which was first picked up by Cheltenham branch. Steve of Cheltenham remembers that it was as a result of some early surfing on his part that the need was first recognised. In November 1993 he tapped into various communities on the internet and discovered that many people seemed to want to share their deepest emotions in this forum. Such confidences received sympathetic responses from some but drew ridicule from others, especially if a person confessed to suicidal feelings. This was clearly an area for The Samaritans. Mike Haines the director, with Steve and others, set up a small working group. The first test was announced on a UK system on 14 July 1994 in the following form: *"Please send us a test message saying how you are feeling (even if you are OK at the moment) and one of our trained volunteers will reply."* Steve recalls that *"within half an hour we got our first message. After three days we'd seen 51 and a few of those really needed to talk. Even those who were not in distress were very welcoming. We were one of the first organisations to take internet users seriously."*

The resulting confidential e-mail befriending service soon showed its potential for reaching out to a new group of callers. Initially this was thought to be likely to appeal mainly to younger people, but as computer literacy has grown, it may now reach every age-group, including the *silver surfers*. It has brought a new dimension to the work since a large proportion of e-mail contacts, maybe as many as 50 per cent, are from outside the British Isles. Some are clearly identified, but in other cases clues are to be found in the use of words and phrasing.

For many branches the new concept was initially approached with great caution. When it was first mooted, there were large numbers of volunteers who would be intimidated by the idea of computer befriending. By the turn of the millennium however, the idea had really taken off and many centres were either on-line, or in process of setting up e-mail befriending. The actual mechanics of dealing with e-mails are very simple since there is a national software package which leads the befriender step by step through the process. E-mails have to be answered with the same kind of awareness as letters. They may be kept by the caller and pondered over for a long time. This means that special training is needed, not so much on how to work the computer (which is what volunteers expected), but how to convey in one message which could be part of an extended *conversation* the warmth and support the caller seeks. It is becoming obvious that the need is infinite, and that the more centres come on-line, the more demand will increase. Where e-mail befriending is offered, the computer terminal will ideally be found alongside the telephones since the needs of these callers are as important as those who contact by more traditional means. It is clear that jo@samaritans.org has come of age.

Another breakthrough in technology has allowed the transfer of phone lines between one centre and another. This has allowed a new approach to staffing centres. In the 1970s it was an absolute *must* that centres provided a 24-hour service. How this was achieved might sometimes seem to a modern eye as rather dubious since transfer of calls to the homes of volunteers at night and other times was, as we have seen, common. When the Elgin branch was set up in 1973 it was sternly admonished that it would only be allowed to open if it provided full cover, although it was the branch with the smallest catchment population in the organisation. This was proudly achieved, despite having only a couple of dozen volunteers at times. In these circumstances, single manning was the only perceived possibility.

In the early 80s the Council passed a resolution that all branches must be available for 24 hours per day on pain of being reduced to a *probationary* branch. The demand was further increased to an insistence on double-manning for the whole of that period, though the sanction about branch status was quietly dropped. This placed a very heavy strain on many smaller branches and they often questioned the need to have two people on duty. There were sound reasons for insisting on this as an essential. One volunteer had actually died while on duty alone, others had been taken ill and there were even in the past a few cases where volunteers had behaved in an unacceptable fashion while on duty overnight, such as inviting friends in and taking the phones off the hook. Needless to say, any such behaviour resulted in immediate and summary dismissal. Another compelling reason was that a volunteer coping with a particularly traumatic call, alone, perhaps at night, with no support, would be in an impossible situation.

The coming of improved telephone services has allowed a complete re-evaluation of the demands on the service, leading to the conclusion that while there are times in a 24-hour period when every possible line needs to be available, predictably the hours of late evening till the small hours of the morning, there are others when the need is much less, notably the early morning. Nowadays branches can transfer their lines to a neighbour or receive someone else's according to the resources they have. This idea was received with caution by many, who saw it as *the thin end of the wedge*, but it seems to be working well at the time of writing.

New thinking in the 80s and 90s allowed places which had seemed to be far too small or remote to sustain a branch to set up operations. In fact these were the very areas which probably had most need of communication channels. Caithness in 1980 and Shetland at Lerwick in 1985 were two such set up in the Scottish region, while Wales produced Llandrindod Wells. Kilkenny and Drogheda opened in Ireland in 1995 and 1997 respectively. Two further tiny and remote island branches, Orkney and Stornoway began in the mid-90s. Stornoway volunteers proudly recall a visit from the Founder when they first opened. They say that when he arrived, he was using a zimmer frame, but by the time he left, he was walking unaided, having benefited from his visit. Some of these branches operate with fewer than 20, sometimes as few as ten volunteers, but they provide a visible presence in their areas. Even if, as in some of the islands, people are shy of making contact with their local centre, volunteers can provide a valuable service to their neighbouring mainland branches by taking their calls when required. This means that 24-hour Samaritan availability in every area is absolute, even if it is not provided by the local branch.

———

Facing the future

Confucius once said *"Study the past if you would divine the future"*. Samaritans may have much to learn from past history.

It seems at first sight that in its early days the movement was a very different animal from its modern counterpart. Current volunteers may be horrified at some of the examples in this brief account illustrating how it was before the organisation knew its limitations. The dramatic stories of members dashing out in the small hours, sometimes alone and unsupported, to a person in danger of self-harm, often through quite dangerous areas of cities; of knives being produced; of bruisers out-facing volunteers and of rescues of battered women may appal. Sometimes more extreme measures might be taken - a shelter offered to a desperate eight-year-old or a safe-house to a reforming prostitute. Heady days, but how dangerous. And what about the premises? Rat-infested, damp and unhygienic, they were often the only place available to start the work, and there are many tales of deprivation and endurance. Nowadays complaints might be made if there are no biscuits or the chairs don't suit. Yet one thing is crystal clear, even if methods were somewhat different, the basic principles and beliefs were exactly the same.

For its first 49 years the movement has been securely founded in the belief in *befriending* and priority has been given to helping those with suicidal thoughts, feelings and impulses. Much has been written and many workshops and training sessions have been presented over the years building on this basic theme. The contribution of many highly talented and committed people, often at the top of their professions helped to shape Samaritan thinking on all the core issues, both in the context of caller care and of volunteer preparation and support. Because of its pioneering work in offering help and support to troubled people and its excellent standard of training, over the years the organisation has earned the respect, not only of medical and psychiatric professionals, but also of other groups concerned to create similar supporting services. From a single Samaritan centre in 1953, there are now 203 in the UK and Ireland and there are over 400 member organisations of the Telephone Helplines Association in the UK, taking over 22m calls between them each year, but it should never be forgotten that The Samaritans was the first, breaking virgin ground.

It would be too easy to assume that by now the thinking is *set in stone*, to feel that what is offered is definitively established. The recent exercise in *Facing the future* has illustrated that the movement should not be complacent or closed to the prospect of change but it has also shown that there are core values which must never be lost. Many *old hands* will very much regret the fact that the word *befriending* on which the whole philosophy developed by the Founder and others in the early days, and on which the work has always been based seems to be out of fashion at present. The phrase *emotional support* has replaced it in the new *Vision and values*. Time will tell whether this will have the same resonance with the public, the callers, or whether Samaritans will simply merge into the general mass of modern help-lines, without distinction. Change may be a good thing and development surely is. History shows that at different periods the emphasis has altered slightly. It seems unlikely that the current developments will be the last. What will the next 50 years bring? Will individual centres give up their identity? Will the service for callers to visit the centres be phased out?

There is one lurking fear in the minds of many. Is there a danger of losing the character of individual branches? Could the service one day be delivered from a call centre? Or, horror of horrors, would there ever be a situation where a caller was answered by a computerised voice saying, *"If you are suicidal, press button three"*? This dreadful prospect has been memorably demonstrated at the York conference in a sketch which emphasises how awful it would be. Liz Reeve, well known to all conference goers as the *Queen of the reception desk*, has often done a brilliant impression of how this would affect a distressed caller. Black humour it may be, but a dreadful warning to be heeded by future generations, as technology marches on. Centralisation in area bases would be feasible in technical terms but the whole ethos of the work would be changed, and an impersonal element, far removed from the warm one-to-one contact which characterises the work at the moment would be introduced.

The most important point to remember is that the movement is unique amongst its fellow helping agencies in that it is run by its own volunteers represented by the Council of Management, the governing body. As long as this is the case, the work should continue in the form that the volunteers want, and in the last analysis it is up to each one to contribute to the ongoing debates about the future as they always have over the last 50 years.

Whatever else there is to be said, the most important person in Samaritan work is, always has been, and always will be, the caller.

A dip into the family album

When an appeal was made for material, a number of kind people made contact. They are generally named as the source for the following notes, though sometimes the original content may have come from someone else. It is hoped nobody will feel unacknowledged.

Some branches have already produced summaries of their own history, sometimes for a branch anniversary. A trawl through a selection illustrates clearly the pattern which was common to many - the initiative of the churches and frequently also the medical profession in the early days, the limitations of the first premises, the kinds of spur which drove the founders to set up their centres and the common threads of care, at first somewhat unstructured but later supported by proper selection and training. Another common feature is the amount of help generally offered by neighbouring branches, though in at least one case the relationship was more suspicious than supportive.

BARNSLEY (North East)

The branch began in 1969 on the initiative of the Christian Council. The early volunteers were all recruited from churches and the meetings were held in the Methodist hall. It was led by Rev. Douglas Drye as director and the chairman and the deputy director were also clergy. (Source: Andy)

BATH (South West)

The rector of Bath Abbey, Rev. Geoffrey Lester called an open meeting of interested parties in February 1964. It is thought that, as in many cases, Chad himself may have suggested it; certainly two speakers came from London. Out of this arose the Bath branch whose first director was Rev. Hayes Treen who led the branch until 1974. The first centre was Abbey Church House, reflecting the close relationship between Samaritans and the church. A founder volunteer recalls that the rector was known as *Batman* as he rushed across from the abbey with his cassock flying out behind him. The early struggles to sort out the premises are described elsewhere. (Source: Mike)

BEDFORD (East)

It was on the initiative of Rev. Stephen Adams the rector of St Stephen's, Bedford that a number of local influential people came together to discuss setting up a branch. They included the head of Bedford School and Jessie Aylett who, as matron, had heard a talk given by Chad in 1958. This group organised a public meeting which was attended by over 100 people and resulted in the setting up of four training meetings. In the early days, volunteers were recruited as *supervisors*, *counsellors*, or *telephone volunteers*. Much help was given by the neighbouring Cambridge branch. The branch officially opened on 14 October 1963 in the garden flat of a large Victorian house. (Source: Fred)

BLACKBURN (North West)

The possibility of a branch in Blackburn was put forward by a working party which included the Dean of Blackburn, a congregational minister and Dr Ramphal and the director of Manchester, Basil Higginson. The branch opened on 1 October 1969, having received the help of neighbouring Bolton in the training of the first volunteers. The town had once been the home of Chad Varah who served a curacy at Holy Trinity Church. In 1996 a blue plaque was placed on the wall of the present centre commemorating the connection.

The branch was set up in the red light district of the town with one emergency line and an office phone. It was directed by Dr Marjorie Fisher, a consultant psychiatrist. In the early days the shifts ended in time for volunteers to catch the last bus. (Source: Joyce)

BOLTON (North West)

This branch was an offshoot of Manchester. At first there was a small group of people, about six, who would be called in by Manchester to befriend someone in the Bolton area. One of these early volunteers recalls his wife taking the calls and himself going out completely alone to see people. The official centre opened in May 1965 in a small room behind the organ in St George's Road Congregational Church. A move to *better* premises meant that volunteers had to climb 50 steps to go on duty. This meant selection owed more to physical fitness than anything else. For many years almost all the overnight calls were taken at home by a lady volunteer who lived alone. The present centre, a terraced house, needed a great deal of work done since it still had the Victorian gas lights and was full of old shoes and clogs left behind by its previous owner, a cobbler. (Source: Roland)

BOURNEMOUTH (South)

Opened 1961. It was founded by Rev. Eric Evans, the vicar of St Peter's Church and his curate, Rev. Eric Read. Like many early branches, selection was rather simplified. One of Eric's favourite recruiting methods was to thrust a copy of *Readers' Digest*, containing an article by Chad into the hands of the potential volunteer with instructions to go away, read it and come back next Thursday. The first activities were in St Peter's parish hall but a move was soon made to

Wooton Gardens. These premises soon proved too small and callers were sometimes seen in strange places, including the bathroom. Further moves had to be made. In the early days volunteers were divided into four categories: consultants, helpers, befrienders and counsellors. Eric Evans was succeeded by Canon Clinch, never known by his first name, only as *the canon*, who lead the branch till 1970, when Rev. Roslyn Aish took over. The clerical tradition here was built into the branch constitution. (Sources: Tony and 40th anniversary booklet)

BRACKNELL (South)

Many volunteers here were inspired by *The Befrienders* on TV. The first director was an Anglican clergyman and the early volunteers were trained at neighbouring Reading. The first call received was the offer of an armchair to the centre. (Source: Olwyn)

BRISTOL (South West)

The idea was conceived in 1963 when the then Bishop, Right Rev. Oliver Tompkins called together six or so volunteers, including two clergy, a housewife, a solicitor and an advertising executive and asked them *"what are you going to do about it?"* This was typical of the process in many places, as the word spread, often through the church network. The branch actually opened in 1965 when interviews were held, and those deemed suitable told to *"report for duty on Thursday week at 10.30"*. The first centre was not far from the current one, but was fairly simple, complete with outside loo. The first director was appointed by the Bishop's committee.

The branch was opened officially by the Lord Mayor who made the first call from the Council House. Those who remember don't think he was suicidal! The branch is now based not far from its origins, in St Nicholas Street. (Sources: Cyril and Dorothy)

CAMBRIDGE (East)

The high rate of suicide amongst undergraduates led a group of dons and clergy led by Canon Edward Maycock to look at the possibility of setting up a group to offer help. It was suggested that it might be called *Suicides Anonymous* or something similar but input from Chad Varah meant that it was set up on Samaritan lines. The branch began in 1962 in two basement rooms overlooking Parker's Piece and was so planned that callers could see the volunteers on duty. This led to one caller refusing to be seen by *"that old school marm!"* The branch was often pro-active in the early days, giving out soup and sandwiches to rough sleepers and sometimes even taking clients home with them. Preparation was in the form of lectures and visits to other organisations such as the Salvation Army. Most early volunteers were recruited from congregations of local churches and the branch was notable for using young volunteers, specifically to keep contact in the university. In its early years Cambridge was not entirely in step with the national organisation, even, in 1967, refusing to allow an official visit from the Executive, but by 1970, under the directorship of Rev. Fred Wilkinson, it became fully integrated. (Source: Vivian)

CHELTENHAM (South and Mid Wales and The Marches)
Canon Hugh Evan Hopkins was the first director here in 1963. Most of the early recruits were clergy or found through churches. The director was aided by his two curates and a lady worker and many of the daytime calls were taken by his secretary. The evenings were covered by volunteers who at that time were quite untrained. Later a system of tapes and lectures provided the preparation for the work. By 1972 the branch was providing full 24-hour cover. In 1996 a generous legacy allowed them to move into their present premises. They have been much helped by an active group of *Friends* and Marjorie, their fund-raising director. Cheltenham has the distinction of being the pioneer of e-mail befriending. (Source: Deirdre)

GALWAY (Irish)
This opened in 1976 in a small four-roomed terraced house. It was considered to be quite large enough for a branch which was expected to be quiet. The increase in caller contacts from 700 in the first year to 7,000 ten years later meant a move to larger premises in 1986. The branch covers a huge area, much of it rural so there has always been a priority on reaching out. A report in 1989 showed a volunteer force of 150, an enviable total to many branches. (Source: *Samaritan News*. 1989)

GUILDFORD (South East)
In 1962 a clergy conference in the Guildford diocese was told about the work of the Portsmouth Samaritans. As a result, the Rev. Colin Pilgrim called a meeting of clergy to investigate setting up a branch. At that time there were only three others anywhere near so it was decided to go ahead. In the earliest days of the branch there was some suspicion about becoming part of a larger movement and even a kind of rivalry with neighbouring groups. It seems that for a while Chad feared they might try to *go it alone*. The founder members of the branch were quite proud of their independent attitude, but by 1965 they

had taken the plunge and become members of *Samaritans Incorporated*, the national body. (Sources: Len and anniversary booklet)

HEREFORD (South and Mid Wales and The Marches)
Influenced by *The Befrienders* on TV the Rev. Burgoyne *(sic)* held a public meeting. This was addressed by Chad Varah and was well attended. The Abbot of nearby Belmont Abbey was enthusiastic and became the first director of the branch, Jerome 32. His fellow monks provided a great deal of help in the early days. At first there were no premises and no money. Volunteers were trained by lectures from such luminaries as Richard Fox and David Evans. Night calls were taken by Worcester branch until they could be handled by Hereford volunteers. Not long after this, they found themselves taking night calls from Shrewsbury - a good example of inter-branch co-operation. (Source: Ruthie)

HORSHAM AND CRAWLEY (South East)
This branch began on 1 May 1973. It was set up on the initiative of neighbouring Reigate which was at that time struggling to cover a huge catchment area. Interviews were carried out in the pews of a couple of local churches and the preparation, carried out by Reigate volunteers, consisted of *"long theoretical lectures"*. It was only at the subsequent ongoing training sessions, which were made fun for the members that the value of interaction and roleplays was *"stumbled upon"*. Horsham Council offered the infant branch the lease on a house which was designated for eventual demolition so the early conditions of work left something to be desired. In Crawley the Council provided a room which could be used for face to face contacts, establishing the presence of the organisation in the town. In 1977 the Horsham centre was opened in its own premises. (Sources: Ben and 21st anniversary booklet)

HULL (North East)
The initial meeting was held as early as 1959 but it was not opened as a branch until 1961, number 14. The initiative came from a number of religious leaders including a rabbi and the head medical social worker at the hospital. Audrey O'Dell, later a well known *character* on the Executive, drew up a training syllabus for the 70 volunteers. The first centre was a cottage lent by Rev. Lake *(sic)*. It was intended to appoint a clergyman as director, in line with other branches but nobody could be found so the branch began without one. Audrey chaired the committee. As soon as it became acceptable to have a lay director, she became the first ever woman to direct a branch. (Source: Audrey O'Dell in anniversary booklet)

KINGSTON (London)

The initiative came from a local vicar, Roger Wild. He recruited four other clergy to deputise for him and Weybridge branch allowed one of their members to transfer and become the fifth deputy, Leila. The initial 174 volunteers were trained by a series of lectures given by Father Aidan Rossiter of Weybridge, a volunteer of great standing in the movement. The first premises consisted of two basement rooms in a house owned by the Girls Friendly Society and a couple of their *old girls* lived upstairs. The emergency number had formerly been that of a laundry and initially many calls were about lost items of washing. Ben Finny, later of Horsham branch and national co-ordinator for work with older people took the first call. (Source: Ben)

KIRKCALDY (Scottish)

In the late 60s two ladies, one a teacher, the other a retired nurse heard a talk given by a Dunfermline volunteer to the local Council of Churches. This inspired them to join. As Dunfermline was some distance away they were often asked to see callers in Kirkcaldy, either in their cars, discreetly parked on the esplanade or in local cafés. Clearly this could not continue so, as a result of a public meeting, about a dozen recruits formed the core of a new branch at Kirkcaldy. They were trained in Dunfermline and a local Church of Scotland minister became the first chairman (Scottish branches do not have directors). A condemned property was put at their disposal and on 10 November 1970, the branch began. By 1975 24-hour cover was available, though, in common with many other centres, much of the night cover was done from home, and the branch was established in improved premises. These were not to be their final destination as the branch has moved several times during its history. (Source: Angus)

LOWESTOFT (East)

In 1965 the Norwich branch was finding itself receiving a larger number of calls from the Lowestoft area than it could handle, so a meeting was organised by the Lowestoft Council of Churches as a result of which 28 people were accepted. These new recruits were bussed over to Norwich for preparation. In the first instance callers answered the calls at home directed from Norwich, but soon they were offered a house by a local church where they began offering increasing hours of cover. By 1972 the first director, Roy, had handed over to Marion and the branch moved to its present premises. Around the same time it became a 24-hour branch. Lowestoft has always been in the forefront of innovative preparation, through the work of Roy which is covered elsewhere. (Source: Neville)

LUTON (East)

The branch began in 1965 and had 80 volunteers in the first year. There was no preparation and volunteers were handed their numbers by the director, Rev. Trevor Nash. It was advertised in the local Chamber of Commerce magazine as *"non-sectarian and non-professional"*. By 1967 it had moved to larger premises and by 1970 was offering a 24-hour service. (Sources: Vi and Rosemary)

MACCLESFIELD (North West)

Founded in 1963 by Rev. Tony Turner, it set up in a condemned house with 25 volunteers. After someone fell through the stairs a move became imperative so the branch moved out to Prestbury into premises found by the local vicar. In 1968 it moved back into Macclesfield again by courtesy of a local minister. In the early days the branch worked in close co-operation with Manchester and some volunteers used to extend their experience by doing duties there. By 1974 a great effort had been made and 24-hour cover achieved. Not long after, Macclesfield was able to help a group in Buxton to set up their own centre. Since the size of the town meant that this would always be very small, by the rules of the period it took Buxton until 1993 to become a full branch though its colleagues in the NW Region always counted it as one of them. (Sources: Hilda and colleagues)

NORTH HERTS AND STEVENAGE IN HITCHIN (East)

This branch began in association with Luton. In common with many others there was a strong input from local clergy. New volunteers were selected and trained by Luton. The first premises, opened in 1971, were in a rent free building in a builder's yard which had no running water or other facilities. At first evening shifts were covered and the key was left at the local pub when no-one was available. 24-hour cover was achieved in 1973. (Source: Margaret)

PORTSMOUTH (South)

The branch was set up in 1961 by the Rev. Bernard Thomas who had been approached by the local casualty department which concerned by the number of attempted suicides it was treating. The original initiative was backed by clergy from all the main Christian denominations, a rabbi and members of the medical and psychiatric professions. The branch started in the billiard room attached to All Saints, Portsea. This was not ideal as clients often had to run the gauntlet of the youth club in order to reach Samaritan help. On one occasion the club members were much entertained by the drama of a woman fleeing from her husband who was brandishing a large knife. In 1964 John Eldrid became director. Much more active befriending was undertaken in the old days, including, on occasion, inviting some callers into the houses of volunteers. (Sources: Jean and Kathleen)

SOUTH DEVON (South West)

Set up in All Saints, Babbacombe in 1965. Early conditions were primitive and cramped. Visiting callers had to sit in the main room where the phone calls were being taken. The branch was impelled to change its premises in 1970 by a visit report which said firmly that callers should not be allowed in the operations room, that the centre was too far out of the main town, and that because it was attached to the vicarage, it was dependent upon any new vicar allowing it to stay. The work was often more pro-active than nowadays. It was even known to provide a Christmas dinner for regular callers. (Source: Kaye)

STAFFORD (West Midland)

In 1963 an open meeting was called by local clergy in response to national publicity about Chad Varah and Samaritans. About 60 local people attended including several clergy, social workers and the governor of the local prison. A steering committee was set up. Preparation consisted of a series of talks by the directors (who were mainly clergy). A semi-religious service was held where the volunteers pledged themselves to Samaritan work with emphasis on the principle of confidentiality. The first premises were shared with a chiropodist, the CAB and Marriage Guidance. Only the evenings were covered and the rest of the calls were transferred to the director's house. 24-hour cover was achieved in 1979. (Source: Tess)

STOCKPORT (North West)

Local interest was aroused by a newspaper headline which read, *"Town of despair"* referring to the high local suicide rate. A public meeting was held in 1975 and a number of recruits resulted. As there were no premises these volunteers had to be trained and do their duties in Manchester. It took four years to find premises since some local people did not want a centre *"in their backyard"*. The derelict house, leased by the council at peppercorn rent was done up as a project by the students of the building department of the neighbouring college. The branch opened in 1979 but was only able to cover two evenings a week as some of their original recruits had become essential to Manchester rotas. Eventually, with help from volunteers who worked in both centres, the branch took off. It moved to its present premises in 1986. (Source: Pat)

TUNBRIDGE WELLS (South East)

Set up in 1966. The first director was the local vicar and the deputies included a Roman Catholic priest and a Methodist minister. The training consisted of six lectures, not about Samaritan methods but rather themes such as psychological problems. In the early days there was more face to face work, much in clients' own homes. In those days, when many did not have a telephone, this was the only way to help. (Source: Jim)

WORCESTER (South and Mid Wales and The Marches)

As a result of discussions with a local consultant psychiatrist, a group of clergy and doctors who were interested in Clinical Theology decided that a practical approach to helping distressed people should be adopted. In 1963 Chad was invited to talk and a group working along Samaritan lines was set up under the direction of the Rev. Stephen Chase. The branch was inaugurated by the Bishop of Worcester who made the first phone call. The *Worcester Evening News* marked the occasion by announcing *"a marriage took place yesterday between technological achievement and human compassion"*. At first the group did not want to be affiliated to the emerging national movement but by the end of 1964 it had become fully integrated. Preparation was a series of four lectures - listening, suicide, mental illness and teenage problems. (Source: Eric)

INDEX

VOLUNTEERS

(By first name ans branch, excluding those who appear elsewhere under their full name, but including some unnamed in the text whose contribution has been helpful.)